Emotional Sobriety
The Next Frontier

Emotional Sobriety
The Next Frontier

Selected Stories
from the AA Grapevine

The AA Grapevine, Inc.
New York, New York
www.aagrapevine.org

ISBN 978-0-933685-57-4

Printed in Canada

Fifth Printing 2010

AA Preamble

Alcoholics Anonymous is a fellowship of men and women who share their experience, strength and hope with each other that they may solve their common problem and help others to recover from alcoholism.

The only requirement for membership is a desire to stop drinking. There are no dues or fees for AA membership; we are self-supporting through our own contributions.

AA is not allied with any sect, denomination, politics, organization or institution; does not wish to engage in any controversy, neither endorses nor opposes any causes. Our primary purpose is to stay sober and help other alcoholics to achieve sobriety.

The Twelve Steps Of Alcoholics Anonymous

1. We admitted we were powerless over alcohol — that our lives had become unmanageable.
2. Came to believe that a Power greater than ourselves could restore us to sanity.
3. Made a decision to turn our will and our lives over to the care of God as we understood Him.
4. Made a searching and fearless moral inventory of ourselves.
5. Admitted to God, to ourselves and to another human being the exact nature of our wrongs.
6. Were entirely ready to have God remove all these defects of character.
7. Humbly asked Him to remove our shortcomings.
8. Made a list of all persons we had harmed and became willing to make amends to them all.
9. Made direct amends to such people wherever possible, except when to do so would injure them or others.
10. Continued to take personal inventory and when we were wrong promptly admitted it.
11. Sought through prayer and meditation to improve our conscious contact with God, as we understood Him, praying only for knowledge of His will for us and the power to carry that out.
12. Having had a spiritual awakening as the result of these steps, we tried to carry this message to alcoholics, and to practice these principles in all our affairs.

The Twelve Traditions Of Alcoholics Anonymous

1. Our common welfare should come first; personal recovery depends upon A.A. unity.
2. For our group purpose there is but one ultimate authority — a loving God as He may express Himself in our group conscience. Our leaders are but trusted servants; they do not govern.
3. The only requirement for A.A. membership is a desire to stop drinking.
4. Each group should be autonomous except in matters affecting other groups or A.A. as a whole.
5. Each group has but one primary purpose — to carry its message to the alcoholic who still suffers.
6. An A.A. group ought never endorse, finance, or lend the A.A. name to any related facility or outside enterprise, lest problems of money, property, and prestige divert us from our primary purpose.
7. Every A.A. group ought to be fully self-supporting, declining outside contributions.
8. Alcoholics Anonymous should remain forever non-professional, but our service centers may employ special workers.
9. A.A., as such, ought never be organized; but we may create service boards or committees directly responsible to those they serve.
10. Alcoholics Anonymous has no opinion on outside issues; hence the A.A. name ought never be drawn into public controversy.
11. Our public relations policy is based on attraction rather than promotion; we need always maintain personal anonymity at the level of press, radio, and films.
12. Anonymity is the spiritual foundation of all our traditions, ever reminding \us to place principles before personalities.

Contents

Preface

IN 1958, THE GRAPEVINE PUBLISHED an article by AA co-founder Bill W. about the ongoing challenges of recovery that he faced long after he stopped drinking. Called "The Next Frontier: Emotional Sobriety," the article describes Bill's insight that his struggle with depression was due to overweening dependencies on other people and outside circumstances. Bill explains how he had found peace of mind by letting go of his expectations and practicing what he calls "outgoing love" — a love less concerned with what one gets and more with what one gives. It was, as he put it, the St. Francis Prayer in action.

For some, the next frontier in recovery from alcoholism may be letting go of faulty, unrealistic dependencies; for others, it may mean illuminating persistent character defects or the "Now what?" malaise that can afflict the long-timer. The stories in this book show that when we have the willingness to find solutions rather than stay stuck in problems, we can let go of fear, selfishness, and resentment, put aside selfish demands, practice outgoing love, and become more connected to our Higher Power and our friends, family, and fellows.

This book does not represent a final definition of emotional sobriety. Growing up in sobriety means different things to each of us, and one's own idea of it may change over time. But one thing seems true: the rewards for reaching for emotional sobriety are serenity, emotional balance, and an increased joy in living.

— The Editors

The Next Frontier:
Emotional Sobriety

January 1958

I THINK THAT MANY OLDSTERS who have put our AA "booze cure" to severe but successful tests still find they often lack emotional sobriety. Perhaps they will be the spearhead for the next major development in AA — the development of much more real maturity and balance (which is to say, humility) in our relations with ourselves, with our fellows, and with God.

Those adolescent urges that so many of us have for top approval, perfect security, and perfect romance — urges quite appropriate to age seventeen — prove to be an impossible way of life when we are at age forty-seven or fifty-seven.

Since AA began, I've taken immense wallops in all these areas because of my failure to grow up, emotionally and spiritually. My God, how painful it is to keep demanding the impossible, and how very painful to discover finally, that all along we have had the cart before the horse! Then comes the final agony of seeing how awfully wrong we have been, but still finding ourselves unable to get off the emotional merry-go-round.

How to translate a right mental conviction into a right emotional result, and so into easy, happy and good living — well, that's not only the neurotic's problem, it's the problem of life itself for all of us who have got to the point of real willingness to hew to right principles in all our affairs.

Even then, as we hew away, peace and joy may still elude us. That's the place so many of us AA oldsters have come to. And it's a hell of a spot, literally. How shall our unconscious — from which so many of our fears, compulsions and phony aspirations still stream — be brought into line with what we actually believe, know and want! How to convince our dumb, raging and hidden "Mr. Hyde" becomes our main task.

I've recently come to believe that this can be achieved. I believe so because I begin to see many benighted ones — folks like you and me — commencing to get results. Last autumn, depression, having no really rational cause at all, almost took me to the cleaners. I began to be scared that I was in for another long chronic spell. Considering the grief I've had with depressions, it wasn't a bright prospect.

I kept asking myself, "Why can't the Twelve Steps work to release depression?" By the hour, I stared at the St. Francis Prayer. . . "It's better to comfort than to be comforted." Here was the formula, all right. But why didn't it work?

Suddenly I realized what the matter was. My basic flaw had always been dependence — almost absolute dependence — on people or circumstances to supply me with prestige, security, and the like. Failing to get these things according to my perfectionist dreams and specifications, I had fought for them. And when defeat came, so did my depression.

There wasn't a chance of making the outgoing love of St. Francis a workable and joyous way of life until these fatal and almost absolute dependencies were cut away.

Because I had over the years undergone a little spiritual development, the absolute quality of these frightful dependencies had never before been so starkly revealed. Reinforced by what Grace I could secure in prayer, I found I had to exert every ounce of will and action to cut off these faulty emotional dependencies upon people, upon AA, indeed, upon any set of circumstances whatsoever. Then only could I be free to love as Francis had. Emotional and instinctual satisfactions, I saw, were really the extra dividends of having love, offering love, and expressing a love appropriate to each relation of life.

Plainly, I could not avail myself of God's love until I was able to offer it back to Him by loving others as He would have me. And I couldn't possibly do that so long as I was victimized by false dependencies.

For my dependency meant demand — a demand for the possession and control of the people and the conditions surrounding me.

While those words "absolute dependency" may look like a gimmick, they were the ones that helped to trigger my release into my present degree of stability and quietness of mind, qualities which I am now trying to consolidate by offering love to others regardless of the return to me.

This seems to be the primary healing circuit: an outgoing love of God's creation and His people, by means of which we avail ourselves of His love for us. It is most clear that the real current can't flow until our paralyzing dependencies are broken, and broken at depth. Only then can we possibly have a glimmer of what adult love really is.

Spiritual calculus, you say? Not a bit of it. Watch any AA of six months working with a new Twelfth Step case. If the case says "To the devil with you" the Twelfth Stepper only smiles and turns to another case. He doesn't feel frustrated or rejected. If his next case responds, and in turn starts to give love and attention to other alcoholics, yet gives none back to him, the sponsor is happy about it anyway. He still doesn't feel rejected; instead he rejoices that his one-time prospect is sober and happy. And if his next following case turns out in later time to be his best friend (or romance) then the sponsor is most joyful. But he well knows that his happiness is a by-product — the extra dividend of giving without any demand for a return.

The really stabilizing thing for him was having and offering love to that strange drunk on his doorstep. That was Francis at work, powerful and practical, minus dependency and minus demand.

In the first six months of my own sobriety, I worked hard with many alcoholics. Not a one responded. Yet this work kept me sober. It wasn't a question of those alcoholics giving me anything. My stability came out of trying to give, not out of demanding that I receive.

Thus I think it can work out with emotional sobriety. If we examine every disturbance we have, great or small, we will find at the root of it some unhealthy dependency and its consequent unhealthy demand. Let us, with God's help, continually surrender these hobbling demands. Then we can be set free to live and love; we may then be able to Twelfth Step ourselves and others into emotional sobriety.

Of course I haven't offered you a really new idea — only a gimmick that has started to unhook several of my own "hexes" at depth. Nowadays my brain no longer races compulsively in either elation, grandiosity or depression. I have been given a quiet place in bright sunshine.

Bill W.

A New Perspective

"Some of us have tried to hold on to our old ideas and the result was nil until we let go absolutely."

– Alcoholics Anonymous, p. 58

Old-timers sometimes say, "Staying sober is simple: Don't drink and change your whole life." The willingness to let go of old ways of thinking and behaving seems to be what emotional sobriety is all about. Once sober, we begin to let go of resentments and fears, self-pity and anger. We try to replace regrets about the past and worries about the future with faith in AA and AA's Twelve Steps and a power greater than ourselves. We used to see problems as insurmountable; now we take responsibility for finding solutions. And we find that, slowly, we can claim moments of real peace — "a quiet place in bright sunshine," as Bill W. puts it in the essay that gave the impetus to this book. For alcoholics, this is a true spiritual awakening.

Growth
June 1976

A NEW THOUGHT has been forming in my mind (now that the AA program has put it in working order). I believe that an element most important in building our sober lives is what is left out.

Several months ago, my husband and I enrolled in a beginners' art course. We didn't become great painters, but both of us now see things, such as leaves and blades of grass and shadings of color, that we weren't aware of before. One day, the instructor showed us a Picasso drawing of the artist's daughter. It pictured her in profile, and it consisted of only three lines. What was left out dramatized what was there. We learned also that in shading a tree, what is left out is as important as the pencil lines, for the blanks create sunlight on the leaves.

It seems to me that I achieve growth by leaving things out — when I don't say the cross word, when I don't answer sarcastically. If I can delay only one second, maybe two, I have time to ask myself, "Do I really want to say that?"

When I wrote down my list of people to make amends to, it was made up mostly of family. I wasn't just thinking of the things I had done. I also remembered the many things I should have, would have, might have done had I not been drinking! The things I had left out ranged from the nice bouquets I could have given, and didn't, all the way to downright neglect.

I used to tell all! To anybody who would listen! And things were going to be my way, too. "Self-will run riot!" Now it's becoming easier to spot ego, and I work at getting the big Me out of the way.

I have discovered a new way to learn — by shutting my mouth and listening. Again, it's not so much what I'm doing as what I'm not doing. I'm not talking. So I'm open; I'm teachable.

I used to like to direct my children's affairs, offering advice when it wasn't wanted and commanding activities and behavior. I'm more secure now. I've thrown out my director's chair. Now, when I see one of my children heading on a certain course and I question the outcome, I keep my mouth shut and practice the Third Step. Whenever there's a problem and I'm involved, I look to see what part of the problem I am causing (as one of my sponsors advised). I'm usually about eighty percent of the problem — well, maybe sixty percent, but the major part, you can bet on that. If I leave out the largest percent (me), there is hardly any problem at all!

I'm becoming so secure in AA, I've even discarded the cute, funny, phony me my civilian friends used to know. I don't have to dance with a rose in my teeth; I can just dance. And I don't have to be the only girl at the picnic who can swing Tarzan-style from a rope into the river. I can swim calmly, like the forty-year-old mother of four I am.

I don't have to show off long legs in a miniskirt any more. I can just sit on them and be happy. And I can say no to a lot of things I'm not interested in. All the people-pleasing activities I used to engage in, I can cut out now. That gives me time to do the truly helpful, gut-warming little things, just because they need doing and I truly care. I have time to work my program.

I can sit quietly and really listen to people trying to communicate with me. My mind is no longer racing to find just the perfect quip to say or story to top theirs.

The eternal internal war I can do without, too. The fighting inside me is over, and am I glad!

And the most important item of all to leave out is the old, familiar foe, alcohol. Without it, life is just plain wonderful!

Tricia J.
Houston, Texas

In All Our Affairs

July 1956

WORDS HAVE A WAY of taking on an entirely new significance when we enter into the new world opened up to us by AA sobriety. We all know how the first apparent clichés of our simple formulas change and become a vital part of our daily life. We discover after a time, for example, that we never really had an inkling of how practically useful "think" is until we accept how very long it has been since we really understood it. "Humility" came, with a bit more sobriety, to take its place as a lovely, living word, a quality of acceptance of our limitations, most devoutly to be searched for; the most desirable member of our family of words — humility.

"Gratitude," that much abused sister, also altered her face and was transformed into a joyful appreciation of our miraculous recovery. We grew to know that without daily gratitude our personal miracle would lose its lustre, and in time it could cover our shiny new world with a–dull–for–granted–taking that would lead us inevitably away from the fellowship and equally inevitably to our most welcoming enemy. We might drink if we became careless with our "gratitude."

"Pride" by a peculiar shift in syntax became the most active and omnipotent devil of a word, perhaps the most dangerous of all, and yet, while unresolved pride can lead us quickly to the bottle, we are tremendously proud that we are a part of AA.

"Honesty — " I heard an AA friend say at a meeting that he had heard a dictionary definition of honesty given by a rural postman at a country meeting in the middle-west. This old boy was sick of hearing this sensible word kicked around so he had gone to the County Court House and looked it up in "that big old dictionary there." It was good enough for him, it's good in any man's life. "Honesty — is the absence of the intent to deceive." Only what does "intent" mean?

Now I find that with all my new-found confidence in the validity and importance of semantics, I have been retarded and stifled by periodic waves of doubt and despair because of my blindness concerning the meaning of the key word to our entire program.

It occurs with perfect rightness in the Twelfth Step: "awakening."

Some hidden closet in my mind had failed to open. To me spiritual awakening meant an absolute conviction of and close relationship to a God everyone seemed to understand but me. I felt, in this untidy recess of my brain, that, without this revelation of spiritual grace, I couldn't begin to "carry the message" adequately and, of even greater importance, I was continually unsuccessful in handling "all my affairs."

I finally looked up the definition of awakening. It means to quicken, to stir, to wake up. It doesn't say anything about a great white light or an aura of divinity, in my dictionary.

Well, now I know without any more fuss or feathers, that I, like every other member of AA, have had a very tangible spiritual awakening. My belief in a Higher Power is as strong as it was when I went to my first AA meeting and accepted the first and second steps as simply and trustfully as a child accepts its mother's milk. And certainly AA with its never ending procession of miracles, has deepened and made tangible the evidence of the workings of that Higher Power. So what on earth was I looking for? I just don't know. I guess I wanted a little Tinker Bell all my own to show me the right and only way out of every situation.

In my peculiarly alcoholic way of creating difficulties, I discovered this semantic truth in the most involved way. Recently I was confronted with a work project that should have presented no particular difficulties, and yet it did. I blocked and blocked and couldn't rationally get around why I was procrastinating, fearful, unable to come to grips with it. I was thinking resentfully that in this year and a half in AA the only departments of my life that had become remotely manageable were my AA activities. I had no feelings of guilty inadequacy after I had been secretary of my group. I met my Grapevine deadlines. I spoke frequently at open and closed meetings. I had done everything requested or required of me without any anxiety as to the perfection of my performances.

Why was I having so much difficulty in the other areas of my life?

Quite suddenly and without any warning bells, the simple solution came to me. I had surrendered to only one thing: my alcoholism. I accepted divine and temporal help in everything that had to do with my disease with complete humility but I never had extended this wonderful freedom from pride, resentments, envy and need for perfection and competition into "all my affairs."

So it finally came to me in this time of really deep need: I had had no understanding of the meaning of spiritual awakening. And because I accepted all things in AA as natural and just and healthy and good, I was only permitting an unconscious use of my spiritual awakening in AA areas. And I had never brought it out and looked at it before.

Now I hope and pray I can indeed carry to all my affairs the conscious use of surrender and humility and gratitude, employing them with the knowledge that, if I do, my affairs, under God's direction have a better chance of reaching a daily truth.

H.W.
Westport, Connecticut

Win Or Lose
August 2001

A S A HARD-CHARGING MARKETER, I used to focus only on winning. I worshiped people like football coach Vince Lombardi, revering him as the patron saint of conquest. So any time one of my victories was less than complete — or, God forbid, I actually lost — my sense of failure was absolute. And this always made me a sitting duck for self-pity — the handmaiden of John Barleycorn.

Joe C., my sponsor, picked up on this soon after we met. He gave me some good advice. "Take the words 'success' and 'failure' out of your vocabulary. Replace them with 'honesty' and 'effort,'" he said.

I wasn't yet ready. I was an advertising hotshot who thought he knew more about competition than did Joe, an electrician at the time. So I continued my Type A behavior and reveled in constant conflict at home and on the job. But his words haunted me for years.

In time, I began to weary of the anger, resentment, and hate fostered by my competitive attitude. One day, another old-timer, Claude W., asked, "Why are you so afraid of losing? Don't you trust God?" Heatedly, I pointed out that, like him, I was in marketing and was paid to succeed.

His response had roots in the same stock Joe had planted years before: "Don't you know that success and failure share a common denominator?" He paused and then really let me have it. "Both are temporary!"

His words have stood the test of time. They helped me to stay sober and to find joy in my chosen profession, with my family and among friends. I thank God, Joe, and Claude for teaching me this lesson in plenty of time to reap its rewards.

Jim M.
Escondido, California

Spiritual Agony
February 2001

M AKING AN AMENDS to the murderer of a precious friend was the most terrifying prospect — next to taking another drink — that I have faced in sobriety. But it also turned out to be the most liberating action I have ever taken sober and the opportunity for which I am most grateful.

My drinking career was short but intense, complete with downing eye-openers on hangover mornings, innumerable blackouts (including a few of the four-day-long, wake-up-in-another-country variety), two car accidents, and four stints in the psych ward, where I detoxed for what I pray was the last time. I was nineteen years old.

I have been sober now for almost two years, and I never cease to be amazed at how deeply the Promises come true for me as I incorporate the principles of our program into my life. However, the first six months of sobriety were enormously painful. I got little relief from the spiritual agony I was in, and, because I did not take the Steps, my compulsion to drink was not lifted.

One chilly October night, as I waited for a ride, shivering and half-heartedly participating in an after-the-meeting meeting, someone suggested that I pray the Third Step prayer and get to work on a Fourth Step. To put it mildly, I balked. I had read the Big Book and sat in enough meetings to know that taking inventory of my resentments — and forgiving those who had wronged me — would play large roles in working the Fourth and Fifth Steps. But because I was, in my mind, the epitome of an innocent victim, I saw no reason to forgive anyone, and I nursed my resentments as if my life depended upon keeping them alive.

Finally I had had enough. My spiritual agony was becoming unbearable. I didn't want to drink again, and without fail, every AA I met with a quality of sobriety I wanted had taken the Fourth and Fifth Steps thoroughly. As one of them put it: "If you want what I have, do what I do." So I sat down and wrote my Fourth Step.

Then in admitting my wrongs to another human being, I was able to see that my resentments had not just been eating my lunch; they had been ruling my life. The people for whom I burned with hatred didn't even know I hated them, and if they did, they probably wouldn't care. My anger was poisoning my soul, not theirs. I wanted to hurt them and was only hurting myself. It was as if I were swallowing rat poison and waiting for those I thought were rats to die. And I was truly surprised that it didn't work.

One especially difficult resentment was a reasonably justified one. When I was a teenager, a dear friend was murdered. He had been an important part of my life and the closest thing I had to a father. When he died, I felt as if I had been dropped into a shark tank with an anvil tied to my foot. "Swim!" the whole world seemed to be saying, jeering at my confusion, loss, and pain.

His killer was found guilty, but insane, and sent to a state mental institution. Imagining the murderer in a paint-chipped ward full of drooling patients in straitjackets gave me some relief. At least she was locked up and in a terrible place, although that wasn't bad enough, of course. The only fitting justice for her was to be slowly tortured to death with my bare hands. And not even that would have satisfied me. I wanted the killer to hurt like I was hurting, and that just wasn't possible.

In the rooms of AA, I found a God of my own understanding, and, with his help, I was able to forgive the person who had caused me this deep pain. But forgiving is not forgetting, and the death of my friend occupied a lot of space in my mind and heart on a daily basis. Though I no longer burned with hatred, the killer was still living in my head rent-free.

I prayed for compassion and received it. One night I was struck with the realization of how lucky I am. All the mistakes I made when I was ill had been repaired to the best of my ability; none of them had been permanent and final. The agony of being responsible for someone else's death is a horrible thing. I learned that in the rooms of AA while listening to people whose drinking led to another's death, usually when they were behind the wheel of a car. There but for the grace of God went I. As an active alcoholic, I was a potential killer every day. That was the truth, and like all truth, it was hard to swallow. I also realized that when my friend's killer was restored to sanity through proper medication for her mental illness, an overwhelming and unamendable regret would be part of her life forever.

A few days after reaching eighteen months of sobriety, I knew that the time had come for me, with God's help, to do my best to set the situation right. I had learned in AA the power of forgiveness and the freedom it offers, both in being forgiven and extending it to others. I wanted that freedom.

My friend was dead; I could not change that. What I could do was make amends for selfishly nursing my resentment. I had burned much energy in useless anger and hatred, and the best way to set that right would be to do what I could to promote healing.

Taking a friend with more than a decade of sobriety, I went to visit the killer in the mental institution. I was clumsy and fumbled my words, but what came out was what was truly in my sober heart: "The person you killed was like a father to me. He meant the world to me. I loved him more than I can put into words. But I have come to a place where it's okay. I used to hate you for taking him away from me, but I don't anymore. I forgive you completely, I sincerely wish you all the best in your life, and I hope you keep getting better. I knew it would be good for me to come here to tell you that, and I hope it will help you to know that someone who loved him very much and was affected really hard by losing him has moved on and forgives you and it's okay."

Grateful that my voice didn't crack and that I didn't get sick from the butterflies dancing in my stomach, I took a deep breath and said a silent prayer of thanks. Then, I sat and watched as the human being in front of me expressed the most sincere sorrow and regret I have ever seen. It allowed me to make peace with my loss. Now I believe that mental illness had robbed this woman of the power of choice, and my friend had died because he was just in a bad place at a bad time.

As I walked down the sidewalk back to my car, I felt the deepest level of forgiveness I've ever known. A 500-pound weight was lifted from my shoulders. I felt free and cleansed. I had just found wings, and they were mine.

Holly H.
Huntsville, Alabama

The Mouth That Roared
August 2001

I ALWAYS TALKED TOO MUCH. Long before I picked up my first beer and long after I put down my last scotch, I talked too much. When I was afraid, I talked to hide my fear; when I felt inadequate, I talked to convince you that I was hip, slick, and cool; when I was in trouble, I talked in such convoluted circles that many times teachers or policemen or sergeants threw up their hands in defeat. I talked so damn much, I got good at it. Or so I thought.

But as my years of sobriety added up, I decided it was time to take a fearless and searching look at this character defect. It was then that I discovered something alarming about myself: in order to fill the air with my words, a lot of what I said was negative. In fact, many of my monologues were little more than verbal volleys against people, places, and things — from the President down to my in-laws, and including my friends and my fellow AAs.

One beautiful fall day, I had a moment of clarity as I was driving with my wife and another AA and his wife. The AA was someone I'd been sponsoring for years. He was also one of the few people who talked more than I did. As we drove along, I began to monitor what he was saying. Here's how his talking went that day: first, he presented the problem, then some dumb so-and-so's solution (which not only didn't work but made the situation worse), then his solution, followed by a series of events that proved his solution was the only successful one. When a new topic sprang forth, my pigeon would listen for a while — but not too long. Then he would begin his cycle all over again.

Listening to him — I mean really listening to what he was saying — opened my eyes (and my ears) to what I'd been doing all these years. As I listened to him, I heard myself. If you sponsor people, you'll never need a mirror.

As soon as I realized this, admitted I was powerless over my tongue, and took a fearless look at the defect, the solution came: if I only said positive things, I'd be talking half as much.

From that day in the car, I've tried to live by this simple edict. When I start badmouthing someone, I quickly curtail my tongue. I've gotten in a lot less trouble since then. (And since I've shared this with my pigeon, he has too.) Oh, I have slips. I revert to type. Before I know what I'm doing, I'll hold forth on so-and-so's latest debacle or so-and-so's program or marriage or whatever. We are not saints. I'll never get this idea down pat. But I'm a better person than I used to be.

The person I used to be is always waiting around the corner. If I close my eyes, I can see him. He's wearing a black leather jacket, smoking a butt, leaning with his back against a building and one knee bent. He's waiting for me to split a six-pack and join him in cussing and complaining and cutting down everything from his ex-boss and the Army to the church, academia, the government — and AA.

But when I close my lips to vicious talk, the old me gets tired of waiting around for someone to commiserate with him. When I say only positive things, the old me disappears. He flips his cigarette into the gutter, turns up the collar of his jacket, and walks away. He just doesn't want to hear it.

John Y.
Russell, Pennsylvania

A Remarkable Sensation
March 1997

I WAS ONE OF THOSE AA newcomers who chafed at the "God parts" of the Twelve Steps. I thought it was beneath my dignity to believe in God. As a budding alcoholic in my early twenties, I had become infatuated with existentialism, a philosophy that contemplates the role of the individual standing alone in an absurd world. Existentialism seemed to dignify my feelings of isolation and uniqueness and to impart a kind of tragic poignancy to the drunken impulsiveness I liked to think of as acts of free choice. When I entered Alcoholics Anonymous, I desperately wanted to stop drinking and to turn my life around, but I was pretty sure I didn't need the help of "God."

However, even during my first days in AA, I was wary of poking holes in the program, lest the whole fabric rip apart. I suspected that if I were to allow myself to make even one exception for myself — such as determining that I would ignore the God Steps — I might open myself to a justification to drink. Therefore, I determined to find a way to live with the whole AA program, including God.

But what did Step Three mean? "Made a decision to turn our will and our lives over to the care of God as we understood Him." How on earth did a person make such a decision? Turning my will and life over sounded like an enormously complicated procedure. And even if I could figure out how it was done, what would become of me if I complied? I worried that by following God's will, I'd end up doing something brave and self-sacrificing — and utterly repellent.

The "Twelve and Twelve" said that the only thing required to take Step Three was "a key called willingness." I thought I was willing. Imagining myself holding this elusive "key," I waited for transformation and felt nothing. The book also compared one's awareness of a higher power to electricity flowing, hidden and potent, through the circuits of a house. But I was unable either to feel the movement of this force or to find the switch that would activate it in my life.

The key finally turned, the electricity finally surged, in a way so quiet and simple I could never have consciously willed it.

At the time I got sober, I had been living with a man for several years. Our relationship had been in trouble for quite a while, and my new sobriety only aggravated our problems, for he felt threatened by my growing reliance on AA, and I was uncomfortable with his continued drinking. I would wake in the middle of the night and discover that he had not come home, and I would fly into a two-pronged panic that he had died in a terrible accident or that he was with someone else. I lay in bed with my eyes wide open, my heart racing until I heard his key in the lock.

One night began typically. I woke, realized he was not home, and felt the fear surface. Then something altogether different happened. I understood that I did not have to follow that route. Without even thinking about what I was doing, I said, not exactly to "God" but definitely not just to myself, "Whatever happens, let me accept it." Instantly a wave of calm washed over me. The panic evaporated. I knew from the core of my being that, because I was sober and was not going to drink over this situation, I was fine. I trusted — something. I fell asleep.

That was sixteen years ago. When I woke up the next morning, I knew I had taken Step Three at last and I was filled with joy. Step Three has continued to manifest in my life in ways that are ever more surprising and profound, for, as the "Twelve and Twelve" promises, "Once we have placed the key of willingness in the lock" and experienced that first opening of the door, "we find that we can always open it some more." Shortly after "turning it over" that night, I broke up with the man I was living with. A few years later I married a man I met in AA. I have stayed sober and continue to go to meetings.

And, interestingly enough, following a spiritual path has become increasingly essential to me. Contrary to my fear that taking Step Three would condemn me to a life of brave self-sacrifice, I find instead that it frees me to think and act as my truest self. My work, which is writing and leading wilderness trips, helps people explore the connection between nature and spirituality. In following this path, my own journey has flowed along several tributaries. Ultimately, however, the entire process comes down to Step Three: I stay sober and turn my will and life over to the care of God as I understand this wise and radiant entity which is manifested in my own soul.

There is an update to this story. One defect of character I battled for years was a bitter jealousy of other writers whom I perceived to be more successful than I. I had worked hard to let go of this chronic ache, but it continued to be easily provoked. A few weeks ago, I did a guided imagery session in which I saw the black, bitter bile of professional jealousy being removed from me by a kindly monkey, who placed it in the earth, where it dissolved and became harmless. A couple of days later my young stepson called to say that his first book had been accepted for publication. I waited for the grip of jealousy, but, astonishingly, felt nothing but happiness for his success.

The next day I reflected on this phenomenon as I drove along the highway in my car. I was thinking about how inner change seems to come only when we are truly ready for it. And then I heard, very clearly, a voice: Are you finally ready to let go and live your destiny?

An old, lingering part of me — that couldn't pass up an opportunity to bargain for what I want — rose up and I thought: Maybe if I say yes, I'll become a famous author.

Yes, I said to the voice.

No, it said. Are you ready to let go and give your life to God?

As often as my Higher Power had addressed itself to me directly in my years of sobriety, it had never before referred to itself as God. Certainly I had never called it that. The fact that it now did so shook me mightily. How could I argue?

Yes, I said simply. I'm ready.

I felt then a remarkable sensation. It was as if my entire body was being emptied of what it no longer needed and was instantly filled with something else. The sensation was of light and energy, a kind of tingling current moving through me.

Here was yet further evidence that AA's miracles can always deepen and crystallize if I don't drink, practice the Steps, and trust the process. As long as I am willing to do what I am called to do in any given moment and to abandon the effort to control the results of my actions, then I am following the path that my Higher Power — call it God, Good Orderly Direction, the soul, the life force, or anything else — has set out for me.

Trebbe J.
Thompson, Pennsylvania

Wait for the Pitch
March 2001

IT WAS THE SUMMER OF 1999, and in order to cover the costs of the October wedding my fiancée and I had planned, I was working as a maitre d', babysitting boozehounds in a fancy gin joint. The money was more than fair, but I hated the job.

I was in my sixth year of sobriety. I knew all about the "actor" noted in the Big Book and his desire to control the elements of production, I was familiar with the key of willingness, and I was aware of the nature of a determined and persistent trial. In my opinion, I had pinned the Third Step to the mat. Still, I suffered tremendous anxiety when I wondered how we were going to pay for our wedding, how I could stomach another night at that job, and how we were going to manage after we got married.

Deep in the throes of this apprehension, a friend who's well-placed in the corporate world offered me four free tickets to an afternoon Yankees game. They were playing my favorite team, the Tigers, and the seats were right behind their dugout, behind third base. It was just the break I needed and I gladly took the tickets. But consternation came on the heels of my acceptance.

None of my buddies could take an afternoon to loll at the ballpark with me. I was stuck with three great tickets, and I didn't know what to do with them. I resolved to turn them over to the One Who Has All Power. I got down on my knees and said I would trust him to figure out what to do with those tickets.

Riding the No. 5 train to Yankee Stadium, I sized up my prospects. Nobody felt right. I continued to place my trust in my Higher Power.

I encountered a man with two children, a boy and a girl, at the box office. Three baseball fans. Three tickets. I asked the dad if he wanted them. I couldn't accept any money (give freely what has been freely given), but I warned him and the kids that they'd be stuck with me for the afternoon. I promised to be on my best behavior, and politely declined his beer offer. A soda, I thought, would be fine.

I got what I came for. It was a tense contest. In a late inning, the Tigers put a man on first, and the next batter took off with the pitch. He lined the ball to right field, and the runner, who'd gotten a terrific jump, was rounding second. The Yankees' right fielder came up with the ball cleanly, but he rushed his throw to third. It landed in the coach's box, kicked off the railing in front of us, and caromed just over our heads. A vicious scramble ensued. The little boy got showered with beer, but his dad emerged with the ball. He handed it to his son, soaked but happy, the proud new owner of a Major League baseball.

A Yankees' beat writer led off his column the next day with that throwing error, the beer-drenched boy, and the dad who retrieved the ball. Reading the reporter's account, I realized that God was the one who brought all that together. It spread out from him, through me. A dad saved some money, a little boy won a souvenir, and a newspaper guy found a lead for his report, because I had trusted that God would show me how to act in this simple situation.

The Tigers, truly awful that year, beat the soon-to-be-World-Series-champion Yankees. Our wedding was a memorable, elegant event for which we received all the help that we needed. I have retired from gin mill work forever, God willing.

Today, I face difficulties that make distasteful jobs and the distribution of free tickets pale in comparison. My greatest challenges are before me. But my experience with the Third Step, even in the smallest matters, gives me the courage to meet whatever lies ahead, twenty-four hours at a time.

Pete P.
Manhattan, New York

The Acid Test

"Then comes the acid test: can we stay sober,
keep in emotional balance,
and live to good purpose under all conditions?"

– Twelve Steps and Twelve Traditions, p. 88

As active alcoholics, we usually responded to a problem by drinking. Then we indulged in self-pity, resentment, fear — which didn't solve the problem. As sober AA members, we can choose a different path, as did the writers of these stories. Instead of giving up, or giving in to despair, these AAs were able to respond to life's challenges and stay sober — and "keep in emotional balance and live to good purpose."

t Was a Dark and Stormy Night

October 1998

MOST OF MY LIFE has been spent on the waters of various oceans. My father was a sea captain, and there were many sailors on my mother's side. Becoming a ship's captain was expected of me. The events I describe here took place in the spring of 1980. I was hired by a company in Anchorage, Alaska, to run their large fishing vessel, the Carole Jeane. I arrived in Seward that spring to pick up the vessel.

My dear friend Vic C. and I had then been in the Fellowship for several years. Vic had kept after me to take him with me on my next voyage in Alaskan waters, so, since he was good with marine engines, he became the engineer aboard the Carole Jeane. After a careful inspection of the vessel we concluded that it wasn't seaworthy, and we spent the next several weeks working on it, trying to get it into seaworthy condition. The owners were very anxious to get the vessel underway though I continually cautioned them about the unsafe condition of the ship.

Meanwhile, in Seward we gathered together several people with drinking problems; this was the start of the organized AA program here. (Today we have at least two well-attended meetings every day.)

The vessel was finally ready. My crew consisted of Vic the engineer, Bob the young cook, Tom the first mate, and myself. We left Seward on a stormy day and the ship's watches were set. Vic and the cook were one team, while Tom and I were on the other watch. The first few hours from port were uneventful. I really felt that we had the vessel under control and things were normal and the engines were operating well.

Then the weather worsened as evening approached, and after dinner I told Vic and the rest of the crew to get some sleep. I'd just returned from the engine room and things seemed to be okay and all systems were go. I picked up a cup of coffee in the galley.

I'd been at the wheel for about two hours when all of a sudden Bob the cook came running up the ladder to the bridge yelling, "We're on fire, we're on fire!" Black smoke followed him. I couldn't believe what was happening. The fire had had a huge start, and at first I didn't realize this. I stopped the vessel so we could concentrate on fighting the blaze. After a few futile minutes of this battle, I realized we were at the mercy of the fire and the vessel was quickly being destroyed. I sent out a Mayday message — the vessel name, location, and the problem; fire at sea. I thought my transmission got out but there was no reply. The vessel's cargo consisted of two large gillnet boats plus 4,000 gallons of aviation gas in drums on deck. We also had 25,000 gallons of diesel fuel in tanks. Many tons of flammable material were stored in the vessel's cargo hold.

I knew we had to abandon ship or we would surely die when the vessel exploded. Tom and Bob found survival suits. Since our liferaft and small boats were on fire, we had lost our main survival gear. The thought of spending a great deal of time in the extremely cold Arctic waters of the Gulf of Alaska was not very comforting. I instructed the men to throw overboard anything that would float. I crawled into my stateroom with a towel over my head to partially shield me from the toxic black smoke. Finally through touch and feel I found a survival suit which I later learned was already damaged by the fire and full of holes.

I can still see Vic jumping into the very cold sea wearing only a life jacket and everyday work clothes. His personal survival suit had been burned by the fire. As we swam away from the fire we found a styrofoam packing case and several timbers. Vic climbed in the packing case for protection from the cold, but the case filled with cold sea water and the situation worsened.

The seas were running from ten to twelve feet, and fog and darkness shut the visibility down to a few yards. Our situation was desperate and we knew it. The two young crew members were very frightened and soon became hysterical. These young men were sure they were going to die in these freezing Alaskan waters. Vic and I decided that the only way we could restore some sort of order and get our crew back to thinking about survival was to have an AA meeting! Can you imagine two members of the Fellowship of Alcoholics Anonymous having a meeting drifting in the Gulf of Alaska on a dark and stormy night, hanging onto a piece of styrofoam? Our two young crew members were spellbound; they stopped their ranting and raving and started to listen to Vic and I talking about how good our lives were and how fortunate we were to have found the AA program. Vic and I were actually laughing as we shared our sober adventures together.

As time passed, Vic became colder and colder, and we had to support his body and keep his head above water to keep him from drowning. After about three hours, a boat light appeared out of the murk. At this time the burning wreck was still afloat and about a third of a mile away. The rescue vessel started a search pattern that took another two hours before their lookout spotted us in the water. After they fished us out, more dead than alive, we began to warm up. Vic was delirious by now so he was wrapped in blankets. I climbed into the bunk with him and tried to transfer my body heat to him.

Our rescue vessel took us back to Seward where we were all hospitalized. Three of us were released the next day, but Vic remained in intensive care for several days because his temperature had been below normal for such a long period of time. Finally he too was released. Vic lived for three more years. He could never work at his old job again. He was never the same.

Vic C. was my inspiration and dear friend. He encouraged me and introduced me to the program of Alcoholics Anonymous. He was my sponsor.

Jack S.
Seward, Alaska

The Value of Life
June 2005

I AM DOING A LIFE SENTENCE in prison because of an alcohol-related accident, one that resulted in the death of an innocent man. So far, I have had several thousand days to re-evaluate my life.

When the shadows of my past were placed in the light, I was thankful for the "design for living" that the Twelve Steps provide. It helps me to handle the shock of who I was, who I am today, and who I want to be. But, even after ten years of sobriety, I find I am just scratching the surface. I have had some very painful moments of reflection on my life and on the actions and behavior that brought me where I am today.

Today, thankfully, a clear and sober mind provides me with the framework to lock my priorities in place. These priorities have become a part of what I consider imperative to the success of my life. But more importantly, they are imperative to the happiness and success of my family. Someone has said that the greatest gift we can give our family is peace of mind; I agree wholeheartedly.

However, once I think I have everything in place and the transformation into my new life is complete, something happens and I am reminded that I am a work in progress.

Three years ago, in my seventh year of sobriety and sixth year of incarceration, I thought I had finally got all my priorities straight. I couldn't have been more wrong.

I was talking to a good friend on the phone, and I brought up the fact that my youngest daughter, Shelly (not her real name), was turning six in a couple of weeks. I explained to him that I was very sad she didn't know what it was like to have a daddy at home. Up to that point, the only daddy that Shelly knew was the one she saw every now and again in a prison visiting room. When she was a baby, I knew I was going to prison for the loss of a man's life, so I memorized every single thing about her and hoped that she would recognize me when she saw me again.

As my friend and I talked, he recognized my despair and wanted to make Shelly's birthday better. He asked me what kinds of things she liked because he wanted to go out and buy her some presents for me. I sat there on the phone in silence because I didn't have a clue what my little girl liked or wanted. I couldn't talk anymore and hung up the phone and went to my bunk and cried. Here I thought I had made all the right changes to ensure my family's happiness, and I didn't know what to tell my friend about my own little girl. I had, once again, discovered that an important priority in my life was missing — not only with my youngest daughter, but with all of my children.

This provided me with the opportunity to make some necessary changes. Sure, it was tough to endure another failure, but in dealing with life on life's terms, I already knew it was going to be difficult at times.

Seven years after my last drink, I still had not become the person I wanted to be. But after weeks and weeks of asking questions and sharing laughs with my little girl, I am a whole lot closer to being that person.

I discovered that everything I thought really mattered no longer did. I found that the little things I took for granted on a daily basis were the things that meant the most. When the fog lifted, and I was standing alone in a strange land, I realized how clouded my thinking had been during my self-medicated haze. I found out, very quickly, that my family was waiting, with hope in their hearts, for the person they knew and loved to return.

As I continue to work the Steps, I write my goals and priorities in pencil, so I can erase them. This is not so I can sell myself short, but so I can strive for more ambitious outcomes. Recovery is a lifelong process; the moment I engrave in stone my blueprint for living, I'll rediscover and recover something that is paramount to the value of my life. And then I'll be looking for a new stone.

Although it is hard not to envy those of you who are free today and can hold your wife and children in your arms and tell them how much they mean to you, I am very thankful to AA and what it has done for my life. In recovery, my life truly does get better, day after day. Each setback I encounter is really just another opportunity in disguise. It is another chance for me to become a better human being. If life can get better for me within the walls of this prison, then I know it can get better for everyone.

Today, I share this Fellowship with recovering alcoholics all over the world who have taken the time to write me and touch my life in a positive way. AA is an amazing Fellowship filled with amazing people. I am constantly humbled by the wonder of it all.

Jeff P.
Blythe, California

Spiritual Coffee-making
August 2001

RECOVERING ALCOHOLICS AND COFFEE seem to go hand in hand — or hand in mug. (If there isn't any coffee when we want it, life can seem very unmanageable!) The spiritual progress of my coffee experience shows how the Steps have helped me improve my relationship with my wife.

Early in my sobriety, I worked nights at the same job that I'd had for a few years. Often my wife would get up before me and start her day. Sometimes she'd be going off to work, sometimes she'd be getting the kids off to school, and other times she would be just doing things around the house. Some mornings, she'd make coffee, and other mornings she'd be content without it.

I would get up after she'd been up for a while and ask if the coffee had been made. Usually the answer was no. This would be cause for much discussion! I just couldn't understand why she wouldn't make the coffee and, if she didn't want it, just leave it for me when I got up. I didn't see how it would take that much effort to make a pot. After several of these discussions, I resolved that there was nothing that I could say that would make any difference anyway, so I wouldn't try to convince her that she should make coffee. I could see clearly that my cries were falling on deaf ears. So I'd get up and grudgingly make the coffee, and we'd sit down and have a cup or two.

Although I stopped mentioning this to my wife, I would often revisit the thought — i.e., the resentment. I knew I was powerless over the coffee being made before I got up, and I began to see the unmanageability of this issue in my life (Step One).

I knew I needed God's help and that he could do for me what I couldn't or wouldn't do for myself (Step Two). I also knew that I needed to take this to God and let him relieve me of my desire for things to be my way. When I prayed the Third Step Prayer, I disciplined myself to really listen to the words "relieve me of the bondage of self, that I may better do thy will. Take away my difficulties, that I may better do thy will." When I heard the words of this prayer, I knew that my difficulty wasn't having coffee ready for me when I got up in the morning. My difficulty was of my own making. This is evident when I am trying to get other people to do things the way I think is best — the way that would best suit my desires.

Next I had to see the selfishness in trying to arrange the show my way (Step Four). I saw this and admitted it to God and my fellows (Step Five). I was convinced that in order for God to remove my defects of character, I first needed to stop practicing my defects of character and doing what wasn't working (Step Six). Then I could humbly ask him for some guidance and direction to see how he could remove these shortcomings, and ask for what would work in this situation (Step Seven). The Seventh Step Prayer states: "I pray that you now remove from me every single defect of character that stands in the way of my usefulness to you and my fellows."

After a few years of sobriety, an opportunity came along for me to relocate to Omaha and work the day shift. As a day-shift person, I had a new routine that I followed every morning. I got up at 5:30 A.M. and made a pot of coffee. Then I showered, brushed my teeth, and got dressed while the coffee was perking. I poured two cups of coffee, one for my wife and one for myself, and while the coffee was cooling (my wife likes her coffee cooled down a little), I said my prayers and did my meditations (Step Eleven). Then my wife and I would have our coffee and conversation before I left for work (Steps Eight and Nine).

I've since moved back to rural Iowa and changed jobs. I still work the day shift and get up before my wife. I still have the coffee made and two cups poured each morning (Step Ten). I still allow time for my prayers and meditations while the coffee cools down. We still have our coffee and conversation each morning. This is as spiritual as life gets for me when I live as though I have had a spiritual awakening as the result of these Steps, and I practice these principles in all of my affairs (Step Twelve).

Last Sunday morning on the way to church with our four children, I mentioned this coffee experience to my wife. My insistence that the coffee be ready for me when I got up was several years ago now, and my wife said she barely remembered these episodes — or discussions as I like to call them. She was touched that I see having coffee with her as a spiritual experience.

I also shared this experience for the first time with my home group last Sunday night. It was a very moving experience that made my eyes leak. (I still have an ego and don't like to say that sharing this experience brought tears to my eyes.)

By the way, this reinforces the importance of a home group where each member can feel at ease sharing experience, strength, and hope. I need my home group to be a place where I can learn to practice the principles embodied in the Twelve Steps with other alcoholics. This sets in motion my willingness to practice these principles in all my affairs, including my home life.

Bill H.
Vinton, Iowa

Winners and Whiners
October 1994

I LOVE THE DIVERSITY OF our Fellowship. I got sober in a small town blessed with three meetings a day, and I have come to appreciate that there are many kinds of meetings — the rough-and-rugged newcomer meetings, the philosophical middle-sobriety ones, and the living-in-the-solution old-timer meetings. I can usually inventory my feelings and needs, then choose the meeting that's right for me. What sometimes happens, however, is that I can selfishly forget which meeting is the right one for service.

I have three sober years now and during the past summer, life was a breeze. When life is easy, I usually assume it's God's way and I'm quite spiritual. But when I'm in emotional trouble, I assume life's a drag and that God's gone fishing. What I've had to figure out is that I can't figure anything out — that when life's a drag, it usually means I'm not living in accordance with the truth that life has its ups and downs. The most difficult part of this phase of my development seems to be my lack of compassion for my own physical and emotional hardships. I kick myself most when I'm down.

Last summer, everything was a snap. I had a terrific job, I was working through close friendships with people in the program, and I was staying in sound physical shape. Then this winter I injured my back, I lost my job, and I've been having a hard time connecting with people. I've been turning my woes over to God on a daily basis; I've been working the Steps; I've been attending lots of meetings; I've been working with my sponsor and sponsoring two great fellows — and yet I'm still living in fear and having physical, spiritual, and emotional blues. The idea comes easily to me that I'm not good enough or that I'm not lovable or that I deserve misery.

My life is so uncomfortable now, and there seems no sign of change, and yet I know from those around me that time takes time. My growth has always been slow and painful. I sometimes have to laugh when that phrase from the Promises is read: "sometimes quickly." But it helps me to remember that the phrase that follows is, "they will always materialize if we work for them." What I notice most is that I am not drinking — a miracle when I consider that people have gone out under similar circumstances — and that I am talking about my feelings. And I am well aware that alone I cannot solve my problems, but that with God and the Fellowship, I can keep growing and living.

So these days, I go to all the meetings. I work with newcomers at the rough-and-tumble meetings to remember what it was like when I got here; I go to the philosophical meetings because I need to hear how people are staying sober; and I go to the stay-in-the-solution meetings because I need to celebrate my sobriety and give myself a break. There are winners and whiners, and sometimes I seem to embody both. I am, as my friends remind me, a human being.

After three years, I'm finally arriving at the second half of the First Step: my life is unmanageable. (They say that if drinking won't bring you to your knees, sobriety will.) But I want to avow that through it all — and I'm always reminded that it hasn't been that long, it just *seems* long — the Fellowship of Alcoholics Anonymous has never failed me.

Gabby H.
Port Townsend, Washington

Faith in Full Flower
November 2003

YESTERDAY WAS MY WEDDING DAY. I have been in this relationship for twenty years now, and the decision to finally tie the knot was prompted by the rapid physical decline of my wife's twenty-four-year-old granddaughter. She has cancer and is not expected to live more than a few weeks at best.

The hastily planned ceremony was held in her hospital room, with five generations of immediate family in attendance. A startled but good-naturedly cooperative social worker also got swept up in the celebration, and a camera was put in her hands to help record the event for posterity, with its light moments and poignant ones.

The vows and rings were exchanged at the foot of our granddaughter's bed, and her young son got to participate as the ring bearer. At one point, he had to crawl under the bed to retrieve my ring, which my nervous bride had dropped before she could get it on my hand.

After the ceremony, we served a simple cake purchased that morning, and a couple of bottles of sparkling apple cider to toast the marriage. For the toast, I asked my granddaughter to offer a few words. She spoke of how she sometimes felt neglected, and angry at Alcoholics Anonymous for all the time we spent at meetings when she was a child, but was grateful we were sober. She also told us she was glad still to be alive to witness the wedding we had put off for so long.

Somehow, it didn't seem strange to anyone there that the wedding was not held in a church, or a park, or someone's backyard. It seemed perfectly natural to bring together a family for a joyful occasion, even in the midst of preparing for a season of grief.

I tell you all this for a reason. Our book Twelve Steps and Twelve Traditions states that "well-grounded AAs seem to have the ability, by God's grace, to take these troubles in stride and turn them into demonstrations of faith."

I am not certain if I have accepted the fact that our granddaughter is about to die, but for some strange reason, I am not afraid. She has a strong faith in God, hopefully as a result of watching us grow spiritually in Alcoholics Anonymous. I believe that, if God ordains that her work is done, we should not try to keep her here. We need to show her that our willingness to accept his will does not apply just to the mundane things in life, but even to the death of a loved one.

When I was sober a year, my grandmother passed away, and I did not handle it very well. I made some mistakes that have yet to be rectified, and which cost me my relationship with my own mother. I now have many more years' experience trying to "practice these principles," and so hope to do things very differently this time.

Butch M.
San Diego, California
Epilogue: Everyone present agreed that our wedding day was our granddaughter's last "good" day. She passed from our sight and hearing six days later.

The Scariest Thing
June 2006

THE SCARIEST THING I EVER did was get sober. Living without alcohol thrust me into a world as alien and threatening as a Martian landscape. For thirty years, the bottle had been my worst friend, my dearest enemy. It was my companion, my keeper, and its loss left me shaky and alone — and afraid. I was afraid of you. I was afraid of me. I was afraid of a God I wouldn't even acknowledge. And I was terrified I would drink again.

So I was very careful. Hugging my fragile sanity close, I moved gingerly through the days. Like a refugee crossing a swift stream, I felt for solid footing step by step. Away from home, I felt I had lost my skin. I saw scorn in every eye, rebuff in every gesture. In my apartment, I sat reading at my kitchen counter, although the open living room was a half-dozen steps away. Somehow, on the comfortable sofa I might relax, lose purpose, drink.

The group I joined saved my life, was my life, is totally integrated in my life today. I took my fear to meetings and sat mute, listening. For an hour, I was safe. For an hour, I had a haven among those whose fear had once been as great as my own. I did not give my fear away — they took it. They eased it from my grasp with hugs and laughter, with shared experience.

Slowly, I became less brittle. I found I need not die nor go crazy. I learned to live with the one I feared the most — myself. Since those days over a decade ago, I've had my life seriously threatened by an auto accident, then cancer. But nothing about death is quite as scary as the exhilarating terror of trying to accept life.

Barbara D.
Carlsbad, California
Barbara died on November 10, 2005. She'd been sober twenty-six years.

Freedom From Self

". . . the alcoholic is an extreme example of self-will run riot . . ."
– Alcoholics Anonymous, p. 62

As active alcoholics, most of us are self-centered, and when we come into AA, our behavior can be still motivated by selfishness, self-seeking, self-pity, and self-centered fear. As we stay sober, however, we get released from "the bondage of self," as the Big Book puts it. We no longer have to be at the center of the universe. We learn a little humility. We give up the idea that the world must always respond promptly to our demands. We cease trying to run the show — ours and everybody else's. We stop playing God — and it turns out there is relief and freedom in that.

Lonely at the Top
May 1991

WHEN I FIRST GOT SOBER fourteen years ago, I had no trouble finding a sponsor. Just about everyone in the group had been sober longer than I had, so all I had to do was find someone who was active and with whom I could relate. My first sponsor was a New York Bowery bum. I related to his low bottom because I too had taken alcoholism just about as far as one can and still survive. He had been sober for ten years when I came to AA, and at the time that seemed to me an eternity. Now, some years later I frequently am the person with the longest time at the meetings I attend.

My second sponsor told me, "The longer you are sober, the narrower the path." At two years' sobriety, I thought this was nonsense. There will come a day, I thought, on which everything will be clear, and I won't have difficulty with the program. I heard one old-timer who said when he was on a rampage, "It is lonely at the top."

Last year, our groups had three people with over twenty years of sobriety who died. In a small town, these people had been truly larger than life and we had depended greatly on them. My sponsor was one of those three. He was in great pain from rheumatoid arthritis, and he suffered from emphysema. After his wife died, he began to rely on me and other sponsees for physical as well as emotional help.

During that time I began to suffer panic attacks. I had been a mental and emotional disaster most of my life with several mental hospitalizations, including electric shock treatment when I was twenty-five, and although AA and God removed these extreme problems, even thinking that they might return was a great threat. One night after a meeting I talked to a newcomer who was having problems. Like anyone else who has stayed sober for a while, I knew things to say that would help him feel better. He told me that I had a wonderful program, and I went home depressed enough to think about suicide. It's lonely at the top.

I need sponsorship, and I especially needed it then. My sponsor was too sick to talk to me very often, and I just didn't want to burden him further. I began to look for another sponsor and ran up against the brick wall — the available pool of sponsors mostly had been sober for less time than I had been. I began to discover that being on top is not just lonely, it hurts. The next day I called up an alcoholic who had been sober a mere five years and asked him to be my sponsor, even though he was the pigeon of one of my pigeons. Like me he had recovered from severe mental problems, and I could relate to him. I also later asked someone with only three years in the program.

I believe that I have been far more teachable with the last two sponsors than I have ever been before. My new sponsor, just having finished a Fourth Step himself, encouraged me to work on one and to follow the section in Alcoholics Anonymous closely and carefully. I had done Fourth Steps before, but somehow had never been willing to follow instructions. It seemed to me, with my long-term sobriety, that I had better behave myself with a less experienced sponsor.

I certainly do not encourage using a sponsor who has just gotten sober, but after a year or so, anyone with a good program should be able to sponsor anyone else. I also do not subscribe to the statement that "the person who got up the earliest this morning has the most sobriety" — length of sobriety has brought me lasting benefits, and I have been more productive and comfortable than I ever dreamed I could be. But I still have no seniority — I am always one drink away from a drunk. I still need help, and sponsorship is an important part of the help that I need. I hear alcoholics bragging about how long their sponsor has been sober. It is good to remember that the length of sobriety is his, not theirs.

I hope that I no longer need a prestigious sponsor. I need help more than prestige. I am in AA for the long haul, and if I am to stay sober longer and longer, there are going to be fewer and fewer alcoholics who have been sober longer than I have been. I don't foresee outgrowing my need for help. I am good at talking to troubled alcoholics — I have sponsored a large number of people. But I have never mastered the art of self-sponsorship, and I doubt that

I ever will. What I need in a sponsor is one who is moving away from a drink, who actively works the Steps, and who is actively involved in the program on a daily basis. With those requirements, it is possible for me to find a large number of people with whom I relate. If a sponsor has to have fifteen-plus years, then I may be looking for some time. My sponsor who died said that, apart from staying sober, his greatest priority was to become an ordinary jerk. Having an ordinary sponsor helps me to achieve that noble goal.

S. C.
Harrisonburg, Virginia

Anonymity: A Day at a Time in the Real World
July 1995

WHEN I WAS FIRST SOBER and learning how to pronounce the word "anonymity," I thought it meant simply that we didn't use our last names at AA meetings. That was fine with me; I didn't particularly want the whole world to know I was an alcoholic. Because my drinking pattern included secret bingeing while I was alone, many of the people with whom I associated weren't aware of my alcoholism. They knew that something was wrong with me, but they didn't know what. So in early sobriety, I kept my mouth shut about my membership in AA.

Then, I went through the evangelist phase. I told everybody that I was a recovering alcoholic, whether they cared or not. I was more than a little proud of my sobriety. Anyone who raised an eyebrow in my direction heard all about alcoholism and recovery. What an expert I thought I was after just a few months of sobriety! I was disappointed when I realized that most people weren't interested in my discovery of the wheel. Patiently they heard me out, then turned the conversation to another topic.

After several years of sobriety, I finally reached a balance: I was comfortable talking about my alcoholism to interested people, but I had abandoned my effort to educate the entire state of Alaska. Then I got a job as a civilian dispatcher at a police department. During the interview for the job, no one asked me whether I had ever used drugs or drank to excess, so I didn't volunteer the information. I was prepared to answer the question honestly; however, I saw no reason to mention it if no one asked.

I'd been on the job for only a week when I overheard the sergeant talking on the telephone to headquarters. He was discussing the possibility of hiring another civilian for a job similar to mine: "She calls herself a recovering alcoholic. She says she has been sober for four years. She goes to the local high schools to speak to the kids about the dangers of drinking."

My heart stirred with excitement. Perhaps they were going to hire another program person to work with me! But then the sergeant paused, listening to the reply from his superior. He burst out laughing.

"That's right," I heard him say. "We don't need that kind around here."

I froze in my chair. A flush spread up my cheeks and across my forehead. "We don't need that kind," indeed! I was that kind! I could barely contain myself. With every bit of willpower I had, I forced myself to stay in the chair and keep typing. The urge was almost overwhelming to leap onto the desk and scream at that stupid sergeant: "I'm an alcoholic! Look at me! We do recover from this disease. See what a shining example of serenity and spirituality I am?"

As I stayed on working at the police department, I learned that the bad attitude many cops had about alcoholics was reinforced by their experiences in the field. They encountered us when our disease was at its worst. The cops responded to accidents, suicides, homicides, burglaries, episodes of domestic violence, and bar fights — and alcohol figured prominently in most of these. The cops dealt with the wreckage.

Once we alcoholics found recovery, the police rarely saw us. Suddenly we dropped from their lives, while others, still in the insanity of their disease, slid in to take our places. The cops had no time to wonder what had happened to those of us who disappeared. They were too busy trying to deal with the next crime, the next disturbance, the next accident, the next mess caused by a still-practicing alcoholic.

The community of law enforcement officers was one more group of people to whom I owed amends. They, too, had been affected by my actions when I had been out practicing my alcoholism. It was painful for me to probe beyond my righteous anger at their apparent insensitivity to see that I had harmed them. But those police dealt with active alcoholism every day of their lives. To make amends for the stress I had caused police, for the pain I had inflicted, I couldn't just jump up on the table and tell them I was recovering. I had to show them.

I received plenty of practice in living the principles of the program while I was at work. When the police were angry, I had to forgive them for reacting to the insanity of active alcoholism. When they came back to the station from a child abuse call or a fatal car wreck, they were sometimes so angry they couldn't speak. Just beneath their anger, I saw the question in their eyes: "Why?" They wanted the carnage to stop. But the next day, another call would come in. Only the faces changed. I learned to admire the police for trying to bring alcoholics to a bottom, by making them face the destruction of their own and other's lives.

When things were quiet, when no one was angry, I began to speak about my past to some of the cops. Before I opened my mouth, however, I did a quick inventory, to determine whether my reasons for sharing were sound. I talked only when I sensed that what I had to say would help them. If my motives were self-seeking, in order to justify a lousy performance or to call attention to myself or to evoke pity, I kept quiet.

Those I shared with encouraged me in my recovery. One officer voiced a wish that more people would find the fellowship of Alcoholics Anonymous.

"We pass it on whenever someone reaches out," I told him. "But they have to want recovery. When they are sick and tired of living that way, they find us.

When they ask for help, we try to be there for them."

Still, when the emergency calls flooded the police station, I had no time to talk about the program. The cops expected me to do my job efficiently, without excuses. Gradually, I became accepted as part of the team. It didn't matter to them what my past was, as long as I did my job to the best of my ability and didn't ask for special treatment.

Never while I worked at the police station did I broadcast the fact that I was a recovering alcoholic, but neither did I hide it. I valued my anonymity in that situation, not because I feared what the cops would think of me, but because I wanted to break it only when it might be of benefit to them. I made amends to the police by carrying the message through my actions that we do recover and go on to live responsible, productive, useful lives. The need to leap onto the table and tell them a thing or two disappeared. They found out who I was. And they accepted me.

Kit K.
Sterling, Alaska

We Get What We Get
October 2001

MY LOCAL MEETINGS ARE BIG on this spot-check reminder: you get what you get; it's what you do with it that counts.

From attending AA meetings in Iowa for the two years I spent in graduate school there, I brought home this question to add to my daily Tenth Step checklist: Am I still learning?

These two ideas help counter my abiding discontent with a job my old attitudes construe as being beneath me. Though I feel embarrassed telling new acquaintances what I do for a paycheck, the facts tell a different story.

Ten years sober, newly trained and degreed as a writer, I had plans for a blockbuster that would get my foot in the publishing door. But I needed to pay my bills. I bought a new suit to go to interviews in, came home that afternoon, got down on my knees, and prayed for God's will to be accomplished in my job search.

Not ten minutes later the phone rang. The local hospital, where I'd worked as a janitor between semesters at grad school, wanted to know if I could fill in for staff taking vacations. After a brief meeting with the supervisor, I came away with a permanent thirty-hour position that would pay my bills, provide health insurance, allow me time for meetings, and leave mornings free to write. I wasn't thrilled with the work, but the situation was ... well, unbelievable. And remember: they called me.

Hey, I told myself, I'm sober, I've worked the Steps, I've got humility. I can do this a year, maybe two. And I'll use the new suit if I ever have to apply for a real job.

Fast-forward six years.

The new suit's been to two weddings. An overflowing cardboard carton of mostly unpublished manuscripts fills the bottom of my office closet. Among them are my Master's thesis, my résumé, and copies of applications to every publication within commuting distance and to a few that aren't.

After many schedule changes, several merit raises, ardent, fearful prayer, and incessant angry disputes among the committee members in my head, I am still mopping floors, getting to meetings, doing service work, sponsoring others, and writing in the morning. Recently, after requesting full-time hours, I was approached for running the department. Once again, they asked me. It's a real job, respectable, challenging, well paid, and a genuine contribution to a service-oriented organization. Best of all, you don't have to wear a suit to do it.

I had to tell them my heart is elsewhere. Showing up and doing the footwork is what I needed, not more responsibility. But I appreciated their consideration and might have a change of heart in the future.

I didn't lie. But the truth is that, working the lowest rung of the ladder has shown me some things about myself that I missed in several Fourth and Fifth

Steps: I struggle constantly with control and detachment. Childish grandiosity still goads me to make a moral issue of every little dispute. Some perverse instinct for unhappiness insists that I must be right. Not good management skills. But also not the emotional fiber necessary to handle a demanding job and also continue writing — which I'm determined to do.

The part of my job that always catches me off-guard, though, is the palpable jolt of pleasure I get from little ways to be helpful — to be of service — to others, for which they are so genuinely grateful. My dry or drinking mind, still alive and quacking, tries to avoid those calls, claiming that's not really my job.

But the real litmus test for me is not letting fear and repugnance at close contact with very ill, decrepit, dying people sever my connection with my Higher Power. Whatever sense of victimization, injustice, absurdity, fraud, or bitter irony my sick mind thrived on drunk, my present circumstances force me to confront every workday as a shortcoming I've not yet mastered.

In early sobriety, I'd been through the loss of marriage, business, property, and money. So I thought I knew all about humility. But picture yourself down on your knees, cleaning vomit off the carpet in the ER waiting room. You glance up to see an old flame standing in the corner, cradling her new baby, and trying to figure out if that's really you. Test your ego-detector against that.

Or say you run into the ex, who almost succeeded in taking everything away from you in that hostile divorce. She's coming out of the gift shop with an overpriced stuffed toy as you're sweating two bags of trash out the door. One of you has to give way. You should say something, right? But principles you espouse insist on civility. Maybe restraint of tongue is the best you can do. So you know there's still work needed in that department.

Like the messes other people make, this is what I get at my job. It's what I get paid for. And it's taught me to view the mess other alcoholics make of their lives as a kind of job security.

Sure, I could compose a life more cinematic. That's easy. Give me a paycheck for the writing work I love — no more than I make as a janitor. I'm a humble guy after all. Or make me rich and famous, I don't care. Just leave everything else exactly the same: a loving marriage, fast friends, modest belongings, good health. This is what I tell God when I'm feeling resentful about what I've got.

But then I reach the end of another sober day and ask: So, am I still learning?

Oh, yes, indeed. And I promptly admit it's not all to my liking. But I go to meetings and remember well that, however crucial, getting sober wasn't to my liking either.

That casts the story in a different light. And I thank my Higher Power for giving me the time and determination it takes to stay sober; and also to write this next novel, the one that's going to send me over the top. There's this middle-aged guy, see, who everybody's given up on. But he's got this one really cool idea that . . .

Well, you get the picture.

Ernest S.
York Harbor, Maine

The Root of Our Troubles
December 1979

MANY YEARS AGO, WHEN I was just a small boy, filled with curiosity, I went to my father and asked him what heaven was like. Wisely, instead of trying to describe something no one really knows anything about, he asked me this question: "Suppose you were in the kitchen and found the last piece of a chocolate pie. What would you do?"

"Well, I love chocolate pie," I replied, "so I guess I would eat it."

"But what if you knew your brother hadn't had a piece?"

I was trapped. Now, I could see where his questions were leading me, and this was not going to be what I wanted to hear.

"If you were in heaven," he said, "you would save that last piece of pie for your brother. That's what heaven is like. It's a world where we all share and think of others' needs before we think of our own."

Well, I decided right then and there that I wanted nothing to do with heaven if that was the way it was going to be. Even though a part of me understood how nice it would be if that degree of harmony was possible, another part of me just couldn't give up that last piece of pie. Looking back, I can see that I've spent enormous amounts of my time and energy arranging people, places, and things in order to get that piece of pie. And not until I nearly destroyed myself with alcohol could I see that my way wasn't the road to happiness after all.

Not long ago, in an AA discussion meeting, my sponsor was talking about self-centeredness. He quoted from the Big Book: "Selfishness — self-centeredness! That, we think, is the root of our troubles." My sponsor declared that all of us probably had that phrase underlined in our Big Books. Well, I didn't know if I had or not. Believe me, when I got home that night, I looked it up, and — what a relief! — I had it underlined in my book, too.

But at the time I underlined it, the real significance of the statement had not been clear to me. Sure, I could admit that on occasion I had been somewhat selfish — staying out all night, spending the grocery money on booze — but it wasn't until I finally got around to doing my Fourth Step inventory that I could see how much self-centeredness had contributed to my failure at life. It was on every page of my inventory. I had created a whole universe centered around me and what I expected out of life. I was my own God; therefore, I really had no God. How miserable life was when I saw the world only through my own eyes! I was unable to reach out to others, and they were unable to reach me. The wonderful experience of peace of mind eluded me until I found the program of Alcoholics Anonymous. Self-centeredness is a poison to my emotional system. It frustrates my every effort toward a comfortable and happy existence. A terrible chain reaction begins. Fear sets in. Anger, resentment, and self-pity become my guiding forces. My only escape is to put this awful selfishness aside and become involved with the world around me.

Alcoholics Anonymous is the perfect solution for our selfishness. This program gives us a purpose and a vision of something much greater than self. We work with others daily. We are forced to become involved with the problems of the newcomer. As a result, our own problems just naturally pale in comparison. When I haven't been to a meeting in a while, simply talking to one of my friends always helps.

Discussion meetings are my favorite cures for reducing this magnified image I sometimes get of myself. There is a magical power that works around those tables. I can go to a meeting wound up tight as a drum, and about ten minutes into the meeting, I invariably begin to feel better. Whatever the problem was, it may still be there, but my attitude toward it has changed. Sometimes, the only place on earth that makes any sense to me is a meeting of Alcoholics Anonymous.

But old habits are hard to break. Occasionally, I still catch myself saying something like: "Why is this happening to me?" or "What is it ever going to take to finally make me happy?" Blinded by my selfishness, I perceive things that way. But in truth, I don't believe it takes anything to be happy. It is an inside job, something I choose, or refuse to choose, for myself. Circumstances outside myself have nothing whatever to do with it.

Anytime I feel that life isn't treating me right, and that everything is against me, then I'm trying to play God again. The longer I'm in this program, the more convinced I become that I really have no idea what's best for me. Who would have imagined that becoming an alcoholic would be something to be grateful for? But indeed I am. Had I not become an alcoholic, I would never have found this way of life that I have always wanted so desperately. My surrender to alcoholism was necessary to open my heart and mind to the healing love of God.

When I joined Alcoholics Anonymous, you told me that if I would walk with you, I would be a free man; that I would never have to drink again if I would only follow twelve simple Steps. But, you told me that in order to keep what I had found, I would have to give it away. I would have to work with others, putting their needs before my own. Sometimes, I don't feel like doing this. I'm still a very selfish person. But I know that if I want to remain sober and free, then these are the things I must do. "Above everything, we alcoholics must be rid of this selfishness. We must, or it kills us!"

I know that my life is no longer my own. My life now is in the hands of "a new Employer." Even though I still complain now and then about the working conditions and sometimes have trouble getting along with my fellow employees, it's a great improvement over the way things were when I was in charge. Although I sometimes take my sobriety for granted, I am never ungrateful for it.

Today, I still don't know that much about heaven, but I've learned some valuable lessons about life on earth. For so many years, I had always believed that the important thing was to be able to draw other people's attention toward myself. I felt I had to have this attention in order to establish my self-worth. This was my only means of security. Today, I know that the opposite is true. The real gift of love is to be able to give it to others. The ability to love can never be taken away from me, except by me. When I can get myself out of the way long enough to love another human being, it's the best feeling I know of. I guess you might say it's heavenly, just the way my dad described it many years ago.

B. S.
Dallas, Texas

Ready, Willing, and Almost Able
April 2000

IN MY SECOND YEAR SOBER, my sponsor suggested going back to karate because of the humility I could gain. The idea of going back to karate at forty, a discipline I had started at age twenty-four, was interesting. After all, I'd already earned my brown belt when I was still an active alcoholic. In fact,

I'd done a lot of things while I was still active, including finishing my master's degree, working for myself, smoking two packs of cigarettes a day, and staying in a dead-end relationship.

While I was studying karate, I earned the fourth of five belts in three years. During that time, I learned more than just karate: I also learned what it was like to belong, and gained a sense of self and confidence, all the while in a safe place.

In most karate classes, people sit in a long row across the studio (or "dojo") and are seated in order of their belt color: the beginners (the "white belts") are on the far side of the room, and the advanced students ("brown belts" or "black belts") are on the other side. The colors of promotion in different martial arts vary and in our school went as follows: white, orange, blue, purple, brown, and black. By the time I left karate (at age twenty-seven), I had earned my brown belt, and was sitting on the advanced side of the dojo.

I started again when I was thirty-five years old. My karate teacher welcomed me back with open arms and introduced me to everyone, since I'd been her student from so many years before. I was not allowed to wear my colored belt, however, because I had not trained in seven years. Nonetheless, my teacher seated me among the other brown belts. After a few months, I was ready to wear my belt. However, my teacher was not of the same mind, believing that I should train for a few more months before wearing my belt. I did not think that this was fair, so I showed her and quit.

Fortunately for me, I got sober two years later and started to reclaim my life. What made me hit bottom was being a pedestrian in a hit-and-run accident in a deserted part of the city where I live. It happened while I was in a drunken blackout. I was frightened and never felt so unsafe. At my first AA meeting, I heard the guy at the front of the room say "Sit back and relax; you are in a safe place." I felt safe. There are so many meetings in New York City; I have been to my fair share, but that particular meeting is still my home group, five years later.

During my first year I met my sponsor. She is a woman with so much grace and humility, it still astounds me. I started working the Steps with her.

My Fourth and Fifth Steps centered a lot around childhood — and child-ish — resentments, including at the top of the list, a resentment against my karate teacher for not promoting me as fast as I deserved (in my mind) to be promoted. My sponsor reminded me to include assets in this Fourth Step, and toward the end of this long list was a two-page chronicle of how this same karate teacher gave me strength, confidence, and a sense of self, at a time in my life when there was very little emotional support.

So, here I was, at age forty, ready to enter karate class again. My teacher was glad to have me back again and introduced me to her other students, positively glowing — wasn't it wonderful that I had been her student years earlier and isn't it great that I'm back again? When, exactly, was this humility my sponsor wanted for me supposed to kick in? I got my answer ten minutes later, when all the students went to sit down. I wasn't wearing my brown belt — after all, I was "humble." When I walked over to the advanced side of the room, the teacher gently told me that I had to sit with the beginners and wear no belt. I thought, "This is different than last time. It's also difficult, but it's certainly possible to sit over here for a few months, until I'm permitted to wear my belt again and sit with the advanced students."

I wore no belt and sat with the white belts for eleven months. What amazed me was that after the first three or four months, I began to accept that I was, indeed, in the right place. This time, I was not ready to wear my belt and I was willing to wait. But I was still relearning karate, still feeling stronger, and still feeling the spirituality which flowed in that room. The difference this time was coming to accept that just because I was not allowed to sit with the brown belts did not mean that I did not deserve to be back in karate class. I didn't know this when I was active. Looking back, it is all too apparent when I see how quickly I was willing to quit karate the second time around, although I loved that class, that school, and that teacher.

This was the gift of humility, taken from the Twelve Steps and brought into my karate school. The only two truly safe places I have encountered in my life were my karate classes and AA meetings. And now AA gave me back karate, because after a year, my karate teacher gave me a new brown belt and told me that I had earned the right to wear it.

The school closed one month after I received that new brown belt, with my karate teacher retiring, going after pursuits of her own. Had I not returned to the school when I did, I might have missed this chance to learn the little bit of humility which was offered to me (yes, and the brown belt, too: it's progress, not perfection).

Of all the things that had happened to me during sobriety, the school's closing just made me so clearly sad. Feeling so unhappy, but not talking about it, I finally blurted out in tears at an AA meeting that I had no karate school, and that it had provided me with such a safe haven and now it was gone. I didn't think about whether or not this was appropriate for AA, but I didn't think it would matter, because no one would really know what I was talking about anyway, other than to remind me that I did not have to drink over it. However, after the meeting ended, an AA member told me about his own karate school. I went to check it out. The people at the desk handed me an introductory pamphlet, explaining that the study of karate at their school would not simply focus on the physical aspects of karate, but would concentrate equally on the emotional and spiritual aspects. This sounded very familiar.

I signed up for this school and explained that, although I had learned a slightly different type of karate, I had, after all, earned my brown belt; I hoped they were going to take that into consideration. They said that was fine, and gave me my uniform — complete with its white beginners' belt.

Elizabeth B.
Manhattan, New York

Thoughts on Step Seven*
August 1955

TIME AFTER TIME during my seven years of AA sobriety I have recognized a character defect and have asked God to remove it and He hasn't done it. I have asked why, and for an answer have been driven to an ever more careful consideration of Step Seven. Here I encounter the crucial word "humbly." If I really want a shortcoming removed I am to ask humbly — that is to say, in humility.

What is humility? It became one of the really vital words in my new AA vocabulary, but just exactly what did it mean?

During my first year or so, humility to me meant an absence of pride. "You've got to be cut down to size," an old-timer remarked, and I flared in resentment. Even while protesting, though, I had a hunch he was right, and it soon grew into a conviction. Getting humility was going to be a laborious grinding-down process, a grim, bumpy business of getting rid of pride.

This would mean a reversal of the way I'd been living, and thinking. All my life I'd been given to understand that to have no pride was contemptible. The strongest of all the pleas about my drinking (and in the end the least effective) was: "Have you no pride?" Pride of self and of family, of school, of business or professional affiliation, of social and fraternal contacts, of parents, children, and sweethearts, of prejudices and of locality, of possessions and of physical attributes, of nationality, intelligence quotient and creed — these I had been encouraged by a pride-puffed world to esteem as the highest values. Now I was told they were excess baggage, to get rid of them and be "cut down to size."

The job was slow, and even this long after is only fairly begun. Sometimes I wearied of it, and asked testily what it had to do with staying sober on any given day. But as the humbling stone of truth ground deeper I saw more and more clearly what it had to do with sobriety. Whenever one of my uncountable prides was touched I'd flare in resentment. And prideful resentment, AA's accumulated centuries of collective sobriety was trying to teach me, is an almost certain prelude to a drunk.

The first to go, and one of the hardest of all, was head-of-family, big-boss-around-the-house, or breadwinner pride. During all my drinking I had "prided myself" — literally — on being a consistent provider. I lost no opportunity to toot the theme on trumpet and cornet and beat it out in Morse code on the tom-toms. I was a damn good provider: let all realize this and pay homage.

As is so often the case, circumstances gave me sound help in getting rid of this pride. All in the same year, the industry I'd served for twenty years bounced me out of a job, and my wife of fifteen years, by legal force, tossed me out of my position as head of the family. And now, mind you, I was sober! I had a choice. I could hang on to my pride and enter into an angry war to win back lost prestige. The Big Book warned me against that path: ". . .the rage and the brainstorm are not for us."

Or I could ask "humbly" that my shortcomings be removed. That way I would have to accept good-naturedly the fact that my family and profession could get along perfectly well without me. I just wasn't as important a property as, all this time, I had thought. If they wanted none of me I could no longer, as of old, bully them into line. I'd just have to let them go their ways, and seek other company — AA company.

Before the cutting-to-size approach to humility was ended — or perhaps I should say before it ceased being predominant, as I doubt if it ever entirely ends — the rough diamond of my bumptiousness had had a number of irregularities ground smooth, or at least a little smoother, on the AA wheel. Every kind of "background" pride — physical or mental, social or ethnic, professional or geographic — tended to wither before the fact, clearly demonstrated at every meeting, that men and women completely lacking in these once-important attributes, possessed something of incalculably greater value to me. They knew how to live, and soberly. The more humbly I was willing to listen and learn from them, the more I gained (for from nothing at all to just a little is nevertheless a gain) in humility.

"Who do you think you are?"

This blunt question has the power to snap me back to a saner notion of my relationships to the universe and to other people, every time I seriously ask it for myself. It helps me to an understanding of my "size." Who am I? I'm one of two billion, 500 million people currently trying to make out an existence on the planet. I don't suppose I'm much more valuable to the Creator than any one of the others.

Nevertheless He has accorded me some very special favors. I shouldn't really be here at all. I'm here on borrowed time, on probation. For I'm alcoholic, enjoying an arrestment of a fatal disease. This certainly gives me no license to push people around, or get annoyed with them or rail at them for not being other than as they are. My proper attitude, AA has tried to leach me, is one of simple thankfulness that I'm still around. Perhaps I might even show a little appreciation of that circumstance, in terms of helpfulness. During the times when I'm thinking along these lines I have the feeling that I'm about down to size, and I'm more comfortable.

As the days have rolled into years, I've come to see that there's another and more wonderful aspect of humility than the negative one of getting rid of pride. It's a mistake to regard the search for humility as just the destruction of a prideful shell. When a chick is born the main event is the arrival on the earth of a new kind of life. In the excitement of this fact, the smashing of the shell is all but forgotten. I think our efforts to learn to ask humbly, that is, to attain humility, may be something like that. Certainly there was a period in the hatching when, from the chick's point of view, life must have seemed nothing but an interminable pecking away at an almost impenetrable shell. But finally it breaks, and he's free.

Might it not be a little bit so with us? In recent years I have felt unmistakably the stirring within me of a new and finer and entirely different kind of life. Possibilities for action within this universe have opened up . . . possibilities I hadn't even dreamed of before. May not we, too, know a new freedom once we're broken out of our shells of fears and fixed ideas, of prejudice and pride?

Step Seven will always be to me the humility step. But humility means a little different thing to me, as an older member, than it did when I was brand new. It isn't all shell-smashing now; new life is stirring.

In the actual taking of Step Seven an unexpected dividend comes to the earnest applicant. When we really ask, as the Step suggests, "humbly," our major character defect, pride, is already on the way to being removed.

J. E.
Bronxville, New York

★Originally, this article was run without a title, as part of a series called "Twelve Steps and the Older Member."

It Works at Work
June 2000

A FRUSTRATING MORNING AT WORK drove me to a noon AA meeting where I was called on to share. I unloaded my frustration of working with people who cared only for themselves. A coworker had (I thought) intentionally misled me about the location of a business meeting where, as a trainee, I was to observe him facilitate. This, I thought, was my big chance and he seemed intent on elbowing me out of the limelight. Four years of both college and sobriety had resulted in an unfinished degree and the title of clerk. No matter how hard I worked, nothing seemed to make a difference in either my income or my title. I was ambitious and hardworking but with no direction. I repeatedly asked my sponsor when I would know what direction I should take at work. His response was always, "Just show up and be of service."

After I concluded my whining, Joe D. was called on. He looked at me and said, "Debbie, no one was happier than I was that you worked the Steps. Now why don't you try working the Traditions? Start with the first one."

It was explained to me that to put our common welfare first, I would have to put myself second. Tradition One meant "putting ourselves to the side and working for the greater good." This was not what I expected to hear, but I had run out of ideas and became willing to try doing it differently.

It didn't take long for me to realize that in order to consider the common welfare of my work group, I had to be willing to let go of my resentments toward them, specifically toward my coworker. I had to look for my part in the situation because I knew by this time that people didn't usually avoid me without good reason. I remembered that a couple of times at a meeting which my coworker was leading, I had fired some of my sarcastic-but-funny comments at his expense. The group laughed but I remembered the look in his eyes. No wonder he was avoiding me! He couldn't control what was coming out of my mouth.

I had to clean up my side of the street with him and did so by telling him that I was both aware of and sorry for what I had done and in the future I would make every effort to support rather than embarrass him. I asked him if there was anything I could do to be of service to him. He didn't jump at my offer.

A few weeks later I saw an opportunity to be of service, and I asked him if he'd like me to assist with the design of a presentation layout for the training course he was preparing. It was an important project and one that he had put a great deal of time and effort into. He accepted my offer. This time, I had a different motive than before, designing to meet the needs of the presenter and the audience instead of my own desire to be paid more or singled out for praise. As the design began to take shape, so did my attitudes about my job. I began to experience the true satisfaction of being a worker among workers.

I found that I had an opportunity to help make something that fostered confidence rather than panic in the presenters. I even found opportunities to apply humor into the presentation, not the wicked kind that hurts but the witty kind that can help people feel good.

The week prior to the Big Event, my coworker asked me to accompany him because, as he put it, "I will have more confidence if I know you are there to help if anything goes wrong with the presentation." Imagine that.

As I worked the First Tradition to the best of my ability, I noticed a sense of well-being at work and an increased interest in others. It had never occurred to me before that the results of working the Traditions might be the same as working the Steps.

And the effect of Tradition One continues to amaze me. A few months after the Big Event, my coworker's wife entered the AA Fellowship for the first time. The combination of relief, gratitude, and awe at the power of the AA program washed over me when I realized that my behavior outside of AA could affect, either positively or negatively, a newcomer who had not yet entered our doors. What would they have thought of this program if I had not cleaned up my side of the street and worked Tradition One? Thank God we will never know because my coworker's wife liked what she saw, wanted what we had, and has just celebrated two years of sobriety. It is my privilege to be her sponsor.

What about my career and the title that I had been so anxious to attain? It comes as no surprise to me that my current job is to identify areas of need in organizations and then design information systems that will meet those needs. As for my job title, it will probably change when I complete my degree, somewhere around June 2001. Imagine that.

Debra M.
Richland, Washington

Simple Program
July 1980

A ROUND THE TABLES, SLOWLY AND with love, my AA teachers have done wonders with and for me. Long ago, I lost depression because of AA. Now, that is a marvelous character defect to lose! As days float joyously by, with or without problems, the AA program continues to be fresh and delightful.

Early in the program, I found "ego deflation at depth" to be a goal toward which I would have to struggle, perhaps for as long as I breathed. Everywhere I turned in the Steps, I was faced with my pride. I had to battle — and continue to battle — to get off the center of the universe. I have not let this fight interfere with the beauty of living in sobriety. Rather, it keeps me steadily attuned to the importance of regular and frequent attendance at meetings.

There has been some improvement in the deflation department, I realized the other day. I no longer have to count the stars at night to make sure they are all out there and in their proper places. And so it is with supervising tides, sunrises, and the flow of rivers on either side of the continental divide, along with many other tasks of which I have been relieved.

Not being concerned with these details anymore, I now have latitude to work on more personal items such as lying, procrastination, indecision, lust, remorse, guilt, and so forth. As a result, the quality of life keeps improving. I complete each day knowing that — even if I no longer have much time to spare from meetings, Twelfth Step calls, family obligations, etc. — somehow, the universe is being cared for. What relief one can get from this simple program!

Anonymous

A Program of Action

*"It is easy to let up on the spiritual program of action
and rest on our laurels. We are headed for trouble if we do,
for alcohol is a subtle foe. We are not cured of alcoholism.
What we really have is a daily reprieve
contingent on the maintenance of our spiritual condition."*
– Alcoholics Anonymous, p. 85

Saying that AA is a program of action is perhaps another way of saying it's a program of solutions. Of course we have problems — all human beings do — but we've been given a practical toolkit to help us stay sober in the face of all sorts of challenges. We take action by going to meetings and giving service, by putting the Steps to work in our lives, by reaching out to our fellow AA members, by healing relationships with family and friends, and by connecting with a higher power of our understanding. In these ways, we begin to look for solutions rather than focusing on problems and find we can live peacefully, happily, and to good purpose in the world.

A Benchmark in Sobriety

September 1991

WHEN I ARRIVED AT THE Eighth and Ninth Steps, I found I had an unusual amends to make. I needed to make amends to the entire town I grew up in, for various acts of juvenile delinquency. There was no way of finding individual firemen, policemen, or citizens I may have involved or harmed twenty years before. But I still wanted to make amends in some way.

I first tried writing a letter to the local newspaper, outlining my transgressions of the past, and declaring that I wanted to apologize to the town. The editor refused to publish my letter, saying that such a letter might actually encourage other young people to misbehave.

So I turned the whole thing over to my Higher Power and went on about the business of living in sobriety.

One day, after about a year in the program, I sat down on a park bench to rest. It occurred to me that someone ought to paint the bench, spruce it up. I thought about doing it myself, but I realized I would need a whole bagful of tools, besides the paint, to do a good job. It was too much for me to deal with. So I turned it over to my Higher Power.

Another year had gone by when I sat on another bench in another park and I thought, "Somebody ought to paint this bench!" I realized that over the preceding year I had acquired most of the tools I would need. All I needed to buy was some paint and some brushes.

I bought the needed supplies, assembled my tools, put them all in a large shopping bag, and began to paint park benches. I took it one day at a time, painting one bench at a time.

Over a period of three years I painted about thirty benches in three parks. Some of the benches were getting tough use and those I painted twice. I used a rasp to smooth out coarse edges and sandpaper to roughen the surface of the smooth, weatherworn boards so they would take the paint. I did a priming coat and another day a finishing coat. It took about four hours' work altogether to do one bench.

I want to say that I enjoyed the work. It wasn't drudgery for me. I was out-doors, in the parks, out in the sun and the wind, listening to the birds, watching the squirrels, and sometimes interacting with people in the park.

I never told anyone, outside of AA, that I was doing this to make amends. I just said that it needed doing and I enjoyed doing it. Some people asked if this was required court-ordered community service, and I said, "No, I'm just a volunteer."

Then came a day, after about three years, when it occurred to me that I was done. I had made my amends to the town. I didn't have to do it anymore.

Several years have passed. I still use those parks as a place to sit and rest. Occasionally I see a bench that needs painting and I remember the work I did. But I don't do it anymore. Now the town does it.

If you can't figure out how to make amends, just turn it over to your Higher Power. In time, there will be an answer, there will be a way.

Jack A.
Montclair, New Jersey

Dropout
September 1977

IT WAS SUMMERTIME, AND I was stretched out in a lounge chair in my backyard. Not more than a schoolyard away, members of my home group were animatedly entering their AA meeting hall.

A twinge of guilt grabbed me, as I tried to avoid, for the umpteenth time, witnessing this happy scene of which I should have been a part. A momen-tary longing to join my fellow AA members asserted itself but was quickly dismissed.

Fifteen years before, I was privileged to be a charter member of that group, the greatest of all groups. (Isn't everyone's home group the greatest?) Now, here I was playing Russian roulette with my sobriety. I had not been an active member of my group for more than three years and had almost completely stopped going to meetings.

I became ungrateful, complacent, and irresponsible. How quickly it can happen! "Do I have to continue going to all those meetings, after so many years of sobriety?" I asked myself. Smug over my longevity, I thought I had reached a saturation point in learning how to stay sober. From two meetings to one to zero can happen so swiftly when our thinking becomes distorted by ingratitude.

I became an AA dropout, optimistically pointing to those who stay sober on their own. But, as we know only too well, the do-it-yourselfers have never entered the wonderful world of AA, so consequently they would not have the withdrawal blahs, as I did.

Much of my time now was being devoted to other activities. These were valuable in themselves, but they were divorcing me from my AA activities, which simmered down to conferences, breakfasts, and retreats, but no regular meetings. Soon, there was a resurgence of ego, a feeling that I no longer needed AA. I'd ever be grateful — oh yeah — but I'd go it alone.

Defects of character began to reappear. Some of my actions became excruciatingly embarrassing. When you punch a hole in a wall and you're sober, how do you explain it? Guilty conscience, maybe? And when you cover the damage with a Serenity Prayer from a Grapevine cover, you need to go all the way back to Step Two.

Needless to say, I was treading on thin ice. Aware of this, I accelerated my attendance at special AA events (though I still took part in no regular meeting activity). I was fearful of stretching my umbilical cord of AA security too far. Special events in AA definitely have their place. They're the answer for the alcoholic who has just sobered up and asks, "What am I going to do with all that time on my hands?" But the meeting is where it really is at, and your home group is the hub of all your AA action.

In fifteen years of sobriety, you find a lot of AA friends and acquaintances, and I renewed these friendships sporadically while attending the special events. The warmth of the longtime friendships had cooled a little. Fellow AA members, the finest and most dedicated associates I've ever known, were polite and congenial. Yet I thought I detected an estrangement, not intentional, I'm sure, but discernible. It had crept into our relationship while I wallowed in my absenteeism from regular meetings.

Surely, my abbreviated AA program was headed for a crisis. Then one day I ran into a friend who tendered me an invitation designed to get me going to meetings again. I was intimidated, in a sense; he was a former pro football player, a six-foot-four-inch, 255-pound end. I thanked him for the invitation, made excuses to break up the confrontation, and promised him I'd think it over (big deal).

After considerable deliberation that night, I finally headed for the meeting. Making that decision was like breaking through a brick wall. It seems that alcoholics are always breaking through walls of some kind.

Arriving at the meeting hall, I hesitated outside. My emotions were similar to those I experienced the night of my introduction to AA. It was quite a while before I could feel a part of that meeting, and several weeks passed before I was brave enough to crash through the barrier and attend my home group again.

My mental blocks were unwarranted. The members of the group where my sponsor-via-invitation was serving as secretary, as well as my home group members, were most gracious in welcoming me back. So I embarked upon another quest for continuous sobriety (how grateful I am that it was not interrupted), with a firm resolve that I would never again take an AA leave of absence.

It has been more than three years since my return to AA activity, and I've never been happier in Alcoholics Anonymous. I firmly believe that our happiness in this program is commensurate with our activity or lack of it. I go to at least three meetings every week. It was my privilege to sponsor a man shortly after my return to activity. I'm certain I would have had to turn him over to someone else had I not resumed working the program as it should be worked.

Together, my Higher Power and I have aided Clay to an active career of unbroken sobriety. He's done a great job, not only with his own program, but in helping others, and that's the name of the game.

A lot of wonderful things have happened to me since my AA rejuvenation. I've been privileged to be secretary to a new group, a group chairman often, and cosponsor a few times. Sponsorship, I think, is our biggest dividend. Seeing a family rehabilitated, the kids smiling again, makes the effort all worthwhile.

I still continue my extra AA activity, the special events, but I recognize them now for what they are — the gravy, not the meat.

If there was one major symptom that led to my inactivity and near tragedy, it was a loss of gratitude. I forgot to be grateful for the wonderful gift of sobriety, forgetting also that one of the best ways to express that gratitude is to pass on the program. Making the AA scene regularly assures us of an opportunity to carry out our mandate to assist suffering alcoholics.

E. B.
Newbury, Ohio

Think Small
March 1979

I THINK I HAVE JUST LEARNED something about humility. This puzzling word has bothered me ever since I came into AA just over a year ago. An old-timer said at a meeting that to him humility was truth, and I have just discovered some truths about myself that are humbling and yet give me a great sense of freedom.

The past few weeks, my thoughts have been pretty negative. I've been trying to live up to my own impossible standards, and I've been feeling very sorry for myself because I fall so short of them. But it sometimes seems necessary to think negative in order to get positive.

I am aware, for instance, that I am not and never have been a gourmet cook;

but with the help of my Higher Power, whom I choose to call God, and with a healthy assist from Betty Crocker, I can feed myself and my family. I cannot clean the house in one day; but I can straighten up the kitchen and make the beds.

I cannot be a wise and tender counselor to my three teenagers and one almost-teenager; but I can point out that if they don't do their homework, they are not likely to pass the course; then, I can let them know that, pass or fail, I will still love them. I cannot always be a loving spouse and cheerful companion to my husband; but I can tell him how much more my life means to me because he is in it.

I cannot give anyone the precious gift of sobriety; but I can listen to a newcomer's problems and tell her how it works for me. I cannot teach a religion class; but I can share my spiritual experiences when it seems appropriate to do so.

I cannot do great things; but I can finish the things I start.

I cannot write a book about recovering from alcoholism; but I can tell other AAs about a new insight that has made my life more manageable by leading me to let go of some old ideas. And thank God, these things that I can do today are enough.

A. B.
Lombard, Illinois

What Will I Get Out of It?
December 2003

WHEN I FIRST GOT SOBER, I wanted to keep AA and all that went with it in a neat little corner of my life. I thought meetings were just for keeping me sober. I never thought that I would make it to the Twelfth Step, where I would be "practicing these principles in all my affairs." However, it wasn't long before what I experienced in the Fellowship started to seep into other areas of my life. At first, these were disturbing encounters, but I gradually saw there was much to be learned and applied.

A few months sober, I began to feel very alone and disconnected when I went to my faith community on Sunday. Nothing had changed at church, but I was changing inside. I compared my uplifted spirits and the aura of excitement in an AA meeting to the drabness I perceived in church. (Today I would probably call that drabness peaceful, but I had no tolerance for peace in early sobriety.) I compared the way I saw our congregation leave after the service to the way my AA meetings broke up: in church, we turned and filed out of our pews with little conversation, whereas in AA, we held hands, prayed, and talked to one another at length before leaving the meeting room. I was feeling lonelier each time I went to church.

One particular Sunday, I left the service sad and full of self-pity, feeling disconnected from my fellow worshippers. With all of my newfound, early sobriety "wisdom," I mounted my mental soapbox and launched several hours of alcoholic, obsessive thinking. You know the kind — where your mind picks an idea and chews on it from every angle until it's unrecognizable. By that evening, I had convinced myself that attending church was worthless and vowed never to return. Luckily, I had a husband who expected me to attend with him each week, so I was back at church the following Sunday. In the meantime, I made myself and my family pretty miserable.

Back in AA, I was blessed with a good dose of healthy fear about relapse and was doing everything my sponsor told me to do. I became the coffee maker at my home group, and sometimes served as a greeter, shaking hands and welcoming people as they came in. I baked cakes and cookies to share with my AA friends. The more service I did, the more people I met. The more people I knew, the more conversations I had at meetings. I felt more and more as if I belonged to AA.

Meanwhile, back in church, I decided to apply the same principle: if it worked in AA, why wouldn't it work in church? I became more active, volunteering as a religious education instructor. I enjoyed that, so I branched out into Youth Ministry and joined other committees. The more service I did, the more people I met. The more people I knew, the more conversations I had in church. I felt more and more as if I belonged to my congregation.

Could it be that I was working the Twelfth Step, "practicing these principles in all my affairs?" The greatest wonder of it all was how happy, joyous, and free I had become when I attended Sunday celebration at my church. Gone were my negativity and critical thoughts about the people around me. No longer did I spend Sunday afternoons sulking about not being spiritually fed by the morning service. And the people were suddenly so much friendlier! Or could it be me? It seemed that I was reaping what I sowed in every situation I entered.

Then, around my fourth year of sobriety, I found a spiritual advisor to help me with my prayer life because I wanted to work the Eleventh Step. Although she wasn't a member of AA, she was a friend of the Fellowship and I trusted her completely. After one of our meetings, when we were discussing a group prayer experience we had attended, I commented, "I didn't get much out of it." She became very agitated and said how sick she was of people saying that. "It's not what you get out of it, it's what you bring into it," she stated emphatically. (Here was a person outside of AA who truly understood the importance of ego deflation at depth.) Was I ever shocked! I was expecting some gentle spiritual nurturing, and I felt as if I had just been smacked. I guess I needed that smack to wake me up and help me remember that my experience of worship in my faith community had changed when I started bringing something to it, and how my connection to AA had grown when I brought more to that. Here was an opportunity to go to another level in my sobriety.

At that time, I was finding meetings somewhat burdensome: it seemed as if the same people told the same stories over and over again. Thinking that I was safely sober, I questioned the importance of allotting precious blocks of time to meetings each week. Instead, I could be out living my new, wonderfully sober life. I see now that I could have been headed down the road to relapse. I suddenly thought about how much I owed the Fellowship of AA. It was always there for me when I needed it. Perhaps on the days when I felt complacent about going to a meeting because I thought I was spiritually fit, I was supposed to help another suffering alcoholic by being available at a meeting. It could be that my spiritual advisor was right: it was more important that I bring something to AA rather than simply take from it.

That was a turning point in my sobriety. Instead of always going to a meeting to feel good, there were more and more times when I went to a meeting to do good. Right about that time, a newly sober woman asked me to be her sponsor. I was wondering why no one had asked me yet! I have had the privilege of watching her grow through the past six years. She has even made me a grandsponsor. What joy! In addition to sponsoring her and a number of other women, I have been able to share my experience, strength, and hope with hundreds, maybe even thousands, of recovering alcoholics inside and outside meetings. This wonderful weaving of AA into every area of my life is a far cry from the way I started my sobriety. I also know that it is bringing me closer to aligning my will with my Higher Power's will for me. Thanks to AA, I am living a healthier, integrated life, by "practicing these principles in all my affairs."

Anne S.
Albany, New York

Made Direct Amends
June 1990

"NO, NEVER! I'M WILLING TO make amends to everyone on my list, but not to her. Not to Janice. Not after the terrible things she said to me. She called me a gold digger! She tried to turn her father and sisters and brother against me! As far as I'm concerned, she owes me an amends!"

As I finished my hostile outburst, my sponsor smiled sweetly with her exasperating, all-knowing look. "You may not be ready to make amends now," she said. "But there will come a time when you want to make amends to Janice.

When you are spiritually ready, your Higher Power will find the right time and place. You'll make your amends, and you will feel wonderful. I promise you, it will happen."

I didn't believe her. I couldn't imagine why I would ever make amends to a person who had insulted and offended me. Janice lived a thousand miles away and that was as close as I wanted her to come.

At thirty, Janice was my husband's oldest daughter. She had suffered terribly when her mother suddenly died of a cerebral hemorrhage. Her grief was so intense that she wrung a promise from her father never to remarry and to keep the family home exactly as her mother had left it. She was a devoted (although bossy) sister to her younger siblings. Talented, educated, and beautiful, she was the mother of an adopted son and a devoted member of her church.

I was told that she had many fine qualities, but no matter. She didn't like me and I didn't like her. She took her father's marriage as a breach of promise and vowed never to forgive him or me. When I tried to win her over, she angrily blamed me for alienating her from her family. She wouldn't listen to my drunk apologies and belligerent fuming. She didn't understand that, as a newlywed, I needed time (and plenty of alcohol) to adjust to my new status. It was all her fault! Then, somewhere during the last seven years of my drinking, she stopped telephoning. All communication between Janice and her family stopped.

But my sponsor was right. The time would come when I could hardly wait to make my amends. Making those amends would show the power of Step Nine to heal old wounds and unite loved ones.

By 1986, no one had seen or talked to Janice for almost seven years. She had stopped telephoning her father or the sister and brother who still lived with us. She never tried to contact her other sister, married and living in another state. Instead, she held on tightly to her grudges.

It was a family of grudge-holders. Her grandfather had gone to his grave without speaking to his brother for over thirty years. Her grandmother had refused to speak to her son's ex-wife for over twenty. If you offended once, you were never forgiven. Old slights were recalled and thrown in your face. No one in the family knew how to say, "I'm sorry." No one ever admitted he or she might be wrong.

Into this family I came — a practicing alcoholic on the final, downward plunge. I added my own flaming resentments to the troubles. I covered up my excesses by blaming the family. I drank the alcoholic's bitter brew of anger, resentment, and bewildering despair. In the end, I alienated my stepfamily completely.

That stepfamily was the primary target of my Eighth Step. I was two years sober when I wrote my list and made those first, difficult, direct amends. With newfound humility and dignity, I recognized my part in the angry scenes and hostile home atmosphere. I admitted my mistakes, as best I remembered them. I said those unfamiliar words, "I'm sorry," and I asked for forgiveness. I told each person what I was doing to turn my life around and promised that I would try my best not to offend again. I never mentioned the other person's behavior; I kept to my side of the street.

My husband and my stepchildren were astonished. No one had ever talked to them that way. No one had ever admitted his or her own weakness or failings before. The pattern of blame, excuses, and grudge-holding had left no room for human error or compassion. Miraculously, everyone accepted my amends with grace and good will. But the real miracle was that they began to realize that they could do the same thing toward those whom they had offended. Making my amends set an example in human relations that would be invaluable in the tragic years ahead.

As I saw and felt the healing power of Step Nine, I began to sense true peace of mind. I began to feel right with the world and right with myself. As I crossed off the names on my Eighth Step list and made my amends to each person, I felt stronger, more secure, more in harmony with myself and others.

But something in me kept telling me I had more work to do. I looked at my list again and realized that Janice's name wasn't even on it. I had totally blanked her out of my mind — and out of my recovery.

As I reviewed my drinking behavior, I saw my motives more clearly. I had interfered between Janice and her father. I had contributed wholeheartedly to family arguments. I had purposely alienated Janice — to keep her from intruding into my life and to protect my right to drink as I wished. She had reacted with hurt anger, which let me justify my own self-serving actions. Seeing my own motives so clearly helped me understand the emotional and psychological stress my disease had created.

Now I wanted more than anything to clear away my guilt. I had reached the point my sponsor talked about: the point of spiritual readiness to work Step Nine completely. Now those thousand miles seemed like an impenetrable distance. I asked my Higher Power to help me find a way to make direct amends.

That summer, my husband and I went on vacation to Lake Havasu, Arizona. Soaring desert temperatures became too hot to endure. As we searched the map for a place to cool off, we realized that Southern California was only a one-day drive away. Janice lived near Los Angeles. We telephoned ahead to ask whether our visit would be welcome. Surprisingly, Janice seemed pleased. I now believe that she was as sick of grudges and bitter memories as we were.

Our visit turned out to be a delightful success. For everyone, it was time to bury the past and start over. On the final day of our visit, I asked Janice if I could speak to her privately. In a very sweet and loving manner, she listened while I explained about my disease and how it had affected our relationship. I told her about AA and how the Fellowship was helping me change my life. And I assured her that I would do everything possible to bring the two sides of our family back together. She paused for a few moments, then hugged me warmly and said, "I think what you're doing is wonderful, and I'm proud of you. Now maybe we can be friends." With those words, the past was gone. We could begin again.

For the next two years, family relationships healed. Janice and her father forgave each other and telephoned frequently. Her brother and his wife and children spent two vacations with Janice's family. Her younger sister moved to California and lived with Janice for six months. Although our relationship was cordial, it wasn't the kind of warm, supportive relationship I enjoyed with my AA friends. But I was happy that we were at least speaking.

Then, in January 1988, Janice telephoned to tell us awful news. She had ovarian cancer. At that moment, our friendship changed. Janice asked for my support, and I was completely willing to give everything I had to help her.

During the next twelve months, Janice endured two surgeries and eight chemotherapies. She lost her long, thick hair. She lost weight and muscle. She lost the socially active life she loved. But she never lost her faith. She was an inspiration to me, and I to her. Through the grace of my Higher Power and the lessons I have learned in AA, I was able to share my experience, strength, and hope — and help Janice keep a positive, faith-filled trust.

Janice's family rallied around her. Old grudges were forgotten. She and I talked at least twice a week, every week for twelve anxious months. Her brother talked to her as much, or more, than I did. Her sisters prayed, and they gave as much support and encouragement as they could. My husband and I sent cards and flowers whenever she went into the hospital. We drove our motor home out to California twice and camped out on the street in front of her house. When Janice was joyfully pronounced "cured," we drove out a third time to celebrate.

Warm, loving, bubbling with life, Janice talked about the future the same way a starving person talks about food. She longed for life, for happiness, for wellness. But six months later, she was dead. A reccurrence in the lower intestine. Colostomy. More chemotherapy. Wasting away. Finally, peace.

I still don't understand the terrible grief I feel. But I understand this: because of the spiritual power of Step Nine, I have no regrets where Janice is concerned. The family that wept together in that flower-laden church would not have been there if Step Nine had not worked its healing magic. Making amends started a chain reaction of forgiveness that changed a whole family.

As my sponsor promised me years ago, I learned more from that one amends — the one I swore I'd never make — than from any other person or event in my recovery.

Carol S.
Albuquerque, New Mexico

The Work at Hand
March 1988

THERE'S THE CHIRRUP OF A SPARROW, the rhythmic tak-tak-tak of a woodpecker, and a low, steady roar from the Interstate. I have stopped work for a moment to rest my racing brain and listen to the silence. When I stop thinking, I find that it isn't silent at all. Even out here, miles from the city, life makes itself heard.

Tony and I are building a small studio for a friend. The pay isn't much, not enough to float my sinking financial ship, but it's work. We often must work one day at a time, uncertain of what job will come next. If I don't worry, and just do each job as well as possible, it's enough. Of the little money we do earn, ten percent goes in payments to people or institutions we have cheated or harmed in the past. By following this and a few other simple suggestions, we stay sober and live fairly decent lives.

It was a big, fat surprise to me to realize that I was alcoholic. One month, I was foreman of a construction crew for one of the more prestigious builders in my area. My wife taught school. We were buying a home, a "fixer-upper" with great potential. Sure, I drank a wee bit too much, but our lives were fine, on the surface. One month later, my wife was gone, I was unemployed, and I was an admitted alcoholic.

Tony takes a last drink of coffee, looks at his watch, and tells me it's time to return to work. We are digging footings by hand. It's hard work in this rocky mountain soil, but like many things that are hard or unpleasant, it has compensations. It keeps us strong, and we get to work out-of-doors.

When my wife moved out, I called a mutual friend, hoping that with her acting as a go-between, we could coax her back home. But Lois did not want to talk about how to get my wife to return. She directed the conversation again and again to drinking. She told tales of her own drinking, and I soon responded with tales of my own. She had seen me in my cups, and I could not convince her that I was a social drinker. As we talked, it became clear to me that most of my problems had been caused by my drinking.

She invited me to a meeting that afternoon, and I accepted. She cautioned that people in meetings introduced themselves as alcoholics. Could I say I was an alcoholic? I didn't know then what it meant to be an alcoholic, but I would have claimed I was a zebra if it would help me not to hurt so much.

"I'm James. I'm an alcoholic."

I said it. The A word. I've said it many times since, and I have not had to drink since that September Sunday.

My brain still works overtime. A large part of my recovery has been in learning how not to listen to myself. When my wife moved out, we decided that I should stay in the house we had been buying together, paying her when I could for her relatively small portion of the downpayment. With the job I had then, such payments would be difficult, but not impossible. A few weeks later, the builder I had worked many years for began to hire subcontractors exclusively. I was out of work.

Then began the darkest hours I've ever faced. In addition to inescapable remorse over having driven my wife away, I woke each day to the likelihood of financial ruin. While unopened bills gathered dust, my brain worried over my situation in dozens of variations. Worse, I slipped into the forever syndrome: I was doomed — I always had been, I always would be.

"Don't think about it," Gentleman Jim told me. In the group I attend regularly there are a lot of Jims, so they get nicknames. Jim says that he was nicknamed "Gentleman" because he wasn't one. I was explaining to him how I thought the Fourth Step worked psychologically. After all, I had already been in Alcoholics Anonymous for more than six weeks, and I had been writing my Fourth Step for more than a week. Surely I was an expert.

"Just do it," he repeated. "Don't think about it."

"But that's why we have brains," I argued. "To help us understand the world, and make decisions based on that."

"Your best understanding got you to Alcoholics Anonymous," Jim reminded me. "Just do what's in front of you, don't think, don't drink, and go to meetings."

"Don't think, eh?"

"Don't think!"

I thought about that. Eventually, I began to see that what I had called thinking was not thinking at all but a kind of squirrel cage of doubt and worry that went around the same issues over and over and always brought me back where I had started.

When my life was very good, I thought it should be still better. I looked for angles. I told myself the world was an accident of physics, and therefore each person was free to take as much as he could. For a long time that attitude was moderated by the people I loved. I moderated my grandiose ambitions enough to include them. As my stinking thinking progressed, I cared less and less for myself and almost nothing for the people who were closest to me.

My conscience could not be stilled. I tried myself again and again, and was found guilty each time. I was worthless, aimless, unkind. Each hurt to others joined the slush fund of self-conviction inside me. I began to drink more to cover that darkness inside. My brain continued its fevered pace, trying to find a way out of the endless loop I had created.

I was a successful employee partly because I tried to keep pace with my spinning brain. At night, every night, I could take my medicine. The daily drinking that had begun a few years before as a beer or two to relax me had become a daily six-pack, and sometimes more. Occasionally, I moderated with wine — often a quart or more each night.

A few months before she left, my wife came home from working late and walked onto the front porch where I sat. I was drinking wine from a quart mason jar. The remainder of a half-gallon was in the refrigerator.

"Are you drinking again?" she asked.

"Yeah. But just a couple. I've really started to get my drinking under control."

"But you drink every night," she said. "Every night you drink."

I thought about that briefly and arrived at the only logical solution. Without answering her, I walked to the back porch, where I could drink in peace.

Tony leans on his shovel and looks at me funny. "Are you thinking about your wife again?" he asks.

"Well, yeah, a little," I answer. I feel like I used to feel when my mother would discover five or six missing cinnamon rolls from the dessert tray.

"James," Tony screeches. "I miss my M-16. You should have seen her. Her name was Janice, and she was a beauty. I lost her. Woe, woe." Tony is a Vietnam vet. When he came to Alcoholics Anonymous, his sick thinking was of the terrors of war. He often nails me like this when I get caught up.

While I still drank, there was one conclusion my thinking was not allowed to arrive at. Since the conclusion I avoided — that I drank too much — was at the heart of every problem, my thinking became circular and dishonest. It was like living in a house with a black hole in the corner of each room. No matter where I went, there was a black hole. When I drank enough, the holes went away. By the time I began receiving help, my brain did not work well anymore.

I also ached with guilt and remorse. I was not a big-time operator, but I had hurt the people who cared most for me.

"Well," said Bicycle Bob. "None of us got here because we sang too loud in church." In meetings, people were sharing their own shortcomings with the group, often to uproarious laughter. It was easier to admit my own faults in such an atmosphere. "You're as sick as you are secret," we say, and my goal now is to be an open book.

I am not a saint, as the long list of people I have hurt demonstrates, but I am working on that list, making amends whenever and wherever they come up.

Probably my most satisfying amends was to my high school music teacher. Twenty-five years ago, he loaned me one of his own music books. Out of laziness or greed, I never returned the book. I have moved about fifteen times in the years since, and have owned and lost a lot of books. I always packed and carried that one book with me, though, through all the houses and cities. I had stopped studying music, and the book was merely baggage.

After a little detective work, I found his address and returned the book with a letter of apology. When I did, I became a little freer. I had one less dark secret to think about.

Tony tells me that it's time to go home. I have been in outer space again, thinking, thinking. When I get caught up in that squirrel cage I often make mistakes. Today I was lucky. Tony must have been maintaining good ground control. The footing trenches are squarely cut and right where they are supposed to be. I hear the low roar from the Interstate again. I have landed safely back on earth.

I have fired accidental physics as the creator of my world and replaced it with my own understanding of a loving God. As long as I practice the principles which keep me close to him, and do as well as I can the work he puts in front of me to do, I will get what I need. I no longer have to think about how my life should go. This brings peace.

I am still strapped financially. I have not found work that pays as well as the job I had when I was still drinking. My wife is now my ex-wife, and is already remarried. Those are pretty tough cookies. What I have now is a growing faith that my life is being directed by a Power greater than myself.

It's only when I stop thinking about it, stop trying to run the show, that my life may become as God intends. I still have consequences of my drinking years to live through. While that is happening, my job is to be, like these trenches, squarely cut and right where I am supposed to be. When I do stop thinking about it, I know that I have finally come home.

James L.
Tucson, Arizona

Take My Advice – I'm Not Using It
May 1997

I WAS FEELING RATHER DEPRESSED and called my sponsor and found her in a similar mood. I said, "What shall I do?" At first she said, "I don't know. If you figure it out call me back." Then because she is a loving person, a good friend, and has a terrific grasp of the AA program, she shifted into sponsorship gear and told me to do the following:

1. Wear life like a loose garment.
2. Don't take myself so seriously.
3. Count my blessings.
4. Find another alcoholic to work with.
5. Read the Big Book and go to a meeting.

Then she laughed and said, "Take my advice — I'm not using it."

I called one of my sponsees, and she was also in a negative frame of mind. I addressed her problem and suggested one through five listed above. She said she had a sponsee in a melancholy mood. I proposed that I and my sponsor, she and her sponsee could form a singing group called The Depressions and sing the blues. She was not amused.

Later in the day my sponsor dropped by with another friend for coffee — and what a change! She'd made a Twelfth Step call and taken another alcoholic to a detox. They recounted how she looked like ten miles of bad road, was ill and full of fear and remorse. Suddenly we were all full of gratitude and laughing at the insanity of self-pity and self-imposed depression. We remembered all the pain and confusion of our early days in Alcoholics Anonymous.

The simplicity of this program never changes — what works is constant: trust in God, clean house, and work with others.

Terry B.
Concord, California

Outgoing Love

"Lord, make me a channel of thy peace –
that where there is hatred, I may bring love –
that where there is wrong, I may bring the spirit of forgiveness –
that where there is discord, I may bring harmony –
that where there is error, I may bring truth –
that where there is doubt, I may bring faith –
that where there is despair, I may bring hope –
that where there are shadows, I may bring light –
that where there is sadness, I may bring joy.
Lord, grant that I may seek rather to comfort
than to be comforted –
to understand, than to be understood –
to love, than to be loved.
For it is by self-forgetting that one finds.
It is by forgiving that one is forgiven.
It is by dying that one awakens to Eternal Life."

– Twelve Steps and Twelve Traditions, p. 99

Most of us will never perfectly achieve the ideals
expressed in this prayer, commonly known as the
St. Francis Prayer. But the stories in this section show that
when we are able to practice outgoing love, we can, in the
words of one writer, "start being open to all the gifts the AA
life can bring."

Put Aside Anger
July 1965

IT SEEMED TO ME once that the great trick in learning to live the AA way of life was to put aside anger. I think now that it's rather a matter of learning to love — and serve. I dimly see these days that there is no freedom from a messy inner landscape of greeds and compulsions until somehow, some-way, we are focused on the miraculous fact that we are given the world and all the people in't to love. Shakespeare's Miranda, pure-of-heart if ever anyone was, concluded from the sight of one very ordinary young man that it was a "brave new world" that lay in store for her beyond Prospero's island. I think we see fairly soon in AA that there is to be for us indeed a brave new world — if we will just walk out and live in it with love. Ah, but it's not so easy to do. There is time needed, and that changing we call growth, and a great deal of help from fellow AAs and from our Higher Power.

Almost all of the time the way to live in outgoing love eludes me. So, perhaps, it is not out of the way to keep on working meanwhile against the negative things. I continue to try to eliminate anger. Surely this comes before the birth of love?

As it happened, anger was the first character defect that I came to ac-knowledge that I possess. It rose to the surface for inspection within a matter of weeks after my entrance into the Fellowship. I could see, and dislike seeing, that I went regularly into rages, and between times lived in a kind of cold suspicion of everybody. (How can you love such unsatisfactory people as the world presents: mean, self-serving, fickle?)

When at last I saw how prone I was to childish tantrums (oh yes, dressed up with adult language and force) I saw — and my heart sank — that it was I who was mean, self-serving, and fickle. It was I who was unloveable, and therefore I who was the cause of my anger at life.

This insight was a shock; I felt that the center of my being had been bombed out. But it was a profitable emptiness for once. I've been in rages since, although less frequently, and have forgotten myself with frustration at friends and kin I don't know how many times, but I am never far away these days from the restorative sense that charity begins at home: I must love (accept) myself, at least, so as to be able to stop being angry and start being open to all the gifts the AA life can bring.

Anonymous

Some Long-time Views
March 1984

MAY A SPECIAL SHAFT OF SERENITY shine upon some alcoholic who thought up and shared that pleasant word "long-timer" instead of "old-timer." I must reciprocate with some long-time views!

One month ago, I shared my thirty-fifth AA birthday on a Sunday night at a meeting in Rondebosch. There was no banquet, no bells, not even a birthday cake. The only concession was a tape recording of the talk. But in that hall, love cascaded over me and poured over my wife, Jessie, who, on one unforgettable morning in 1947, beseeched me to write to New York for help when I was dying of alcoholism at the age of twenty-five here in South Africa.

There was no phone number to call; regular meetings were to materialize much later; there was no local box to write to furtively, no material proof in the form of a sponsor to show my trembling vision that AA worked. That was the way it was. That was the way it had to be — for me. I was perpetually terrified, a mass of fluctuating suspicions, so thin-skinned and painfully sensitive to the slightest vibrations of authority that if there had been a nearby AA group or central office, I doubt if I would have made contact with it.

For me at that time, it had to be done through the quiet power of the written word, initiated by Bobby, at the AA General Service Office in New York, and embossed by Ann M., Bill, and Bob, who sent such love in so many letters over many years. As compulsively as I used to drink, I now felt a celestial obsession with AA sobriety, and my exhilaration forced me to write all over the States for any crumbs that they could spare. They sent me whole cakes of indescribable mental richness, iced with humility, laughter, and alcoholic love. After groups were formed here, Bill W.'s guidance often saved us from calamity.

One day, the Big Book (it had somehow been overlooked) was placed in my hands at five in the afternoon, when I arrived home from work. As I recollect, I had been undergoing the early pangs of "monotonous" sobriety that we often feel around our fifth month in AA, when we haven't a clue about the program. There was a cup of tea on the kitchen table, ready. Next to the steaming cup was the book, in a navy blue cover — Alcoholics Anonymous, 1948 printing.

I finished reading this masterpiece at six the following morning. The tea, now cold, remained untouched; the ashtray, empty. I hadn't had time to loosen my tie or remove my jacket. Only once did I leave the table; then, the book went with me to the bathroom. It was the greatest, most artistically crafted journal of recovery, and it still is. I was spellbound by the majesty of the wording, the delicacy of the suggestions, catering to the individuality of each alcoholic. At last, this whole venture made sense! For me, the essence of it lay in the second paragraph on page 164: "He will show you how to create the Fellowship you crave."

I have read this beloved book over and over. It still uplifts, inspires, and guides. Through the years, I have read thousands of books and pamphlets, but the Big Book is still the superstar. The love flowing from its pages encourages me to keep the blade of my sobriety ever sharp and gleaming, to cut through all the ignorance and terror that surround still-suffering alcoholics. When their tears dry and the pain recedes, I see in their eyes the image of God, always illuminating the Fellowship of which I am a part, thanks to him and to all of you.

P. O.
Wynberg, South Africa

An Equal-Opportunity Deplorer
March 1983

ICAME TO AA BECAUSE I was "sick and tired of being sick and tired." By not drinking and by going to a lot of meetings, I achieved the sort of dryness that made it unnecessary to drink — and also unnecessary to discard most of my old ideas and conceptions. I picked a "sponsor" who supported that system.

I was free to not drink, not work well at my job, be as irritating as a hangnail in a pickle factory, and deplore the antics of any and all groups in and out of AA. I was an equal-opportunity deplorer: I felt particular animosity toward motor-cyclists, bankrupts, homosexuals, people who took any kind of drug, divorced people, liberals, ad nauseam. But for some reason, even with all these people to roundly deprecate and feel superior to, I wasn't happy. As a matter of fact, I was very unhappy. I drew some kind of perverse enjoyment from my misery.

I changed jobs and cities. Through a series of adroit and somewhat sneaky moves, my Higher Power let me wind up in an AA group consisting of people who worked hard on the program. With the help of a solid sponsor, I went to work on the Steps, all twelve, in the manner and in the order in which they are explained in the Big Book.

Almost without realizing it, I was losing enough fear and gaining enough faith to feel okay. It was no longer a case of just being sick and tired of being sick and tired; my life changed to such an extent that I was no longer afraid to be "happy, joyous, and free." As I worked through the Steps slowly and some-times hesitantly, my attitudes, my self-image, my relationships with other hu-man beings — virtually everything in my life — changed. I no longer wanted to run out in front of everybody and holler, "Follow me!"

I found that people outside the program could be as loving and sharing as those inside. Times changed; life changed; and people in the program began asking me to sponsor them. God saw to it that I was kept busy; for that reason, I needed to help new people recover as quickly as they were able, so I would have time for others who asked.

Along with that, He began to set me straight on some of those old ideas. I ran into one "bankrupt" who didn't even know that he was. Since joining AA, he has worked off, without legal bankruptcy, tens of thousands of dollars of indebtedness. One by one, they came into my life: liberals, young people, hippies, Bill and his Harley-Davidson, state employees, a tenured professor, gays, and lately, when God so elected, one member who must have some medication to correct his brain so that he will be able to function.

I ask God each morning, "Please take care of . . . ," and I name them all. Each night, I thank him for taking care of every person on the list, which has grown to eighty-five names. Just who is sponsoring whom is in God's hands after a while.

I have learned to begin each of these sponsorships with the statement: "I am willing to love you, to accept you just as you are. I will not judge you nor expect you to do anything just to please me. There are no qualifications on this love. I will never suggest that you do anything I have not done. If you want what people with good sobriety have, then you will do what they have done — the Twelve Steps of this program."

I ask each one to call me anytime he feels like it, to share joys as well as problems. In the past, I sometimes made the mistake of saying, "Call me when you have a problem." The upshot was that I was "teaching" my friends to have problems so they would have a reason to call. Now, we talk over the good and the indifferent as well as the occasional off-the-program days. I have driven my car many a mile, quietly and slowly covering the back roads, sharing and talking, laughing and sometimes crying. These are times of building trust, learning to share, gaining the faith to be "happy, joyous, and free." I gain insights into myself and learn how God wants me to broaden my horizons in the program.

So many things from so many sources have aided me in reaching into myself and others that I cannot always pinpoint just when and where a particular truth occurred to me. However, I want to share what I consider to be two key concepts. The first is that as long as I am acting in a loving and caring manner, I am not responsible for how others react. This frees me from pleasing people at my own emotional expense. The second concept is, I feel, the clearest basis for sharing our insides with another: feelings are neither right nor wrong. It is what we do with our feelings that we should concentrate on.

Through sponsorship, the program taught me, slowly and ever so gently, to love and be loved. It taught me to touch, to walk by a friend and pat him or her on the head and say, "That's just in case nobody gave you a pat on the head today." I learned the value of saying, "You're okay," with a hug. I learned the fun and joy of being childlike, of being able to laugh and enjoy life. I learned life.

As I share what I know of the program and am willing to learn from those with whom I share, I find a deeper and more rewarding contact with God. My understanding changes and broadens through wider and wider exposure to many different kinds of people from varied backgrounds. The one common element that runs through all these relationships is the strong desire to stay sober and to go beyond sobriety to full-fledged recovery.

R. M.
Temple, Texas

As Unique As Ham and Eggs
June 2000

THIRTY-TWO YEARS AGO, IN APRIL 1968, I lay on my bed in a fetal position. I was told by a doctor that he didn't think I'd live through the night. That was where my alcoholism took me. Today this seventy-two-year-old black man would like to share with you where my sobriety, one day at a time, has taken me.

I woke up this morning at about four A.M. The electric clock was blinking at me because the electricity had gone out sometime during the night. Physically, I felt really bad and I hadn't even put my foot on the floor yet. I started thinking, oh my God, here I go again, another diabetic day. Since I've been diagnosed with diabetes, I have days when, for no apparent reason, I don't feel well. So I try to take it in stride, knowing full well that it will pass and that more than likely something will happen during the day to take my mind completely off how I feel, both physically and emotionally. So I get busy and do what's in front of me.

My mind went to my ninety-year-old friend who is in a nursing home. I had promised him I'd take him out today and give him a little relief from the boredom of the place. It's hard for him now because he was always in the know and always with people in downtown Oceanside. He doesn't like to participate in the nursing home activities. He would much rather go for a ride and look at things he can see.

This was on my mind as I rolled out of bed and got myself ready to go to my AA meeting that I attend every morning, except for the days I'm working at our central office. Years ago, I heard a guy share that people were asking him, jokingly, what he was going to do when he retired, and he said: "Get more active in Alcoholics Anonymous." This really stuck with me, so I try to be as active as I can. After our Daily Reflections book came out a few years ago, our Friendship Center started daily morning meetings based on the daily readings. Today the Reflection read: "Frequent contact with newcomers and with others is the bright spot of our lives." I could really identify with the alcoholic who wrote realizing that we are all sort of a garden-variety human being, and the things we get the most joy out of are the things that sometimes we don't want to do. I certainly wasn't thinking about doing too much today other than taking my friend for a short ride.

I picked him up about eight o'clock and we went to the meeting, where we were greeted by a bunch of people who were very grateful they were sober. They were all glad to see him and this made my heart kind of sing, the way they treated him and welcomed him. Both of us have been sober thirty-two years now, my friend and I. Afterwards he wanted to get a haircut. One barber shop was closed and the other one had an hour's waiting time but we took that in stride.

Then we went by the senior care center where he had spent some time and he got an opportunity to talk to some of the social workers and some of the patients there and he was just glowing. I could tell he felt really good and his spirits were lifted. We left there and headed for McDonalds for a grilled chicken sandwich. I learned how to cope with his eating habits because I now have a bib for him to catch all that extra food. I used to get really upset with him when he had his nice clothes on and then he would start wearing his food while eating.

We left there and went back to the old neighborhood, in the Barrio, where we both spent a lot of time. I'm telling you this to show you how things work in our program of recovery. You just do what you know is the right thing to do. The first person we ran into was a little guy we'd met about eight years ago. This little guy has tried to sober up many times: he gets sober for about a week or two and then gets drunk again. He saw my truck pull up and started talking and thanking me for some things I had done for his son and himself. He laid it on pretty thick, so I told him I didn't have any money and not to lay it on so thick, and he got a kick out of that. As we were driving away, my friend said, "Man, you know, he sure has a good head on his shoulders and he's really educated." I said yes, but it doesn't do too much to help keep him sober, just like it doesn't do too much good to carry the Big Book on your arm all day if you don't open it up and read it.

I have been trying many times to talk to my friend about the fact that he's been blessed in so many ways, and that he's just at a place in his life where he cannot do the things he used to do and wants to do. I told him he still has a pretty good life and it's up to him to make the best of it. I try to remind him about the program and that it's one day at a time. So as we were driving away, he said to me, "You know, I really have been in pretty good health." I said, "You're correct about that. As a matter of fact, you've been in pretty good health for about ninety years. It's just that your body is getting older now and giving out on you some."

He said, "Yeah, you're right." I said: "Your biggest problem today is that you don't like where you live. We know some people today who have some very serious health problems. Think about your buddy who's been very active in the community. Now he has to cancel doctor's appointments because he can't get from point A to point B. That has never been your problem and I hope it never is your problem. It won't be as long as God keeps me involved in the Fellowship of Alcoholics Anonymous."

The last thing my friend requested this day was to go by the central office. He knew I worked there and he wanted to see the manager, who is a friend of ours. So we went into the air-conditioned office. As you walk in the door, you see the circle and triangle embossed in the linoleum. My friend saw this symbol and I asked him if he knew what it was all about. He remembered about unity, service, and recovery and the circle being the world. I felt really good about that.

I'm coming to the end of my day now and I just thought it was important to share how my diabetic day got turned around. In thirty-two years I have never, ever had doubts about whether or not this program works. I think I am about as unique as ham and eggs. Frequent contact with others and what I can do today to help others is the answer. It took a long time for me to come to this realization. I thought my problems would be solved if only. If only . . . then I'd be all right. It just doesn't work that way. It takes the little things that happened today — they're not dramatic but they prove my Higher Power works when I don't even think he's working.

I'm home now, sitting here thinking about what a great day I had, from moment to moment. It turned out that just by putting one foot in front of the other and not questioning, I was able to go with the flow. Everything was in God's hands and I really had a good day. It had nothing to do with the excitement of a girlfriend, money, property, or prestige. My friend was the bright spot in my life today, along with all the other people I came in contact with. I can honestly say that I love the old man. I love him for who he is and what he has done for me and others and tonight my heart is full. I never thought that a day like today would be a high point of my life. All that excitement that I used to crave and strive for was not there. I don't have to live on the edge anymore. And tonight as I lay my head on my pillow I can't think of one single thing that I did today that I have to go back and redo and make amends for.

Not bad at all for a seventy-two-year-old tongue-chewin' drunk.

Sam L.
Oceanside, California

Miracle In a Burger Joint
March 2002

O F ALL MY EXPERIENCES in sobriety, none can match what happened the day that the Promises started coming true in my life: it was a Sunday afternoon and I was to meet my estranged wife at a local burger joint to give my children back to her after visiting with them for a day. Our divorce was almost final, she was taking good care of our children and herself, and was moving forward with her life. Unfortunately, I was unable to accept this fact and, more often than not, was filled with fear, anger, and jealousy. These feelings were something I constantly struggled with and had to turn over to my Higher Power on a daily basis. She soon arrived, and as we were taking our food to our table, I noticed the new engagement ring she was sporting. I said, "Nice ring – where did you get that?" She looked at it, smiled and spoke his name. I could feel my blood pressure rise, and I knew that I was about to ruin the day. But instead of preparing to throw my hamburger into her face, to rant, rave, cuss, and generally cause a scene, I silently said that simple prayer that I had become so very familiar with: "God, please help me."

And that is when it happened. At that very moment, my entire world and body seemed to stop. I felt something like warm honey being poured over my mind and body. I closed my eyes and lowered my head as this warm feeling completely covered me. As I opened my eyes to look at my feet, I fully expected to be standing in a puddle of this liquid! Of course, there was nothing there, but something inexplicable had happened because when I looked back up at my ex-wife, the only thing I was capable of feeling was — are you ready for this? — love. That's right — love.

Not romantic love or any other kind of love that I've ever known or felt, but a love that I can only describe as coming straight from God. A love born of complete and total acceptance. And at that very instant, I suddenly realized that God was doing for me what I could not do for myself.

My life has not been the same since that day. And in the seven years since then, the Promises have continued to come true for me. I love sobriety and I love life. And I have my Higher Power, the Twelve Steps of Alcoholics Anonymous, and my brothers and sisters in recovery to thank for it. The Big Book says that the Promises "will always materialize if we work for them." I believe it.

Lester W.
Oceanside, California

The Ability to Love
May 1962

SINCE MY FIRST DAY IN AA I have been hearing about love as manifested in our Fellowship. I heard the members talk about the privilege of making Twelfth Step calls, the love they felt for drunks. I sat through these meetings, nursing the shame that I did not always feel this.

In trying to work the honesty part of the program, I had to admit that I did not always like to call on drunks and that I had little tolerance or patience with them. I accepted the calls because I had been taught from the beginning that my sobriety depended upon it. There was also an element of fear — if I refused to take calls, I would be criticized by the group, and their approval was of utmost importance to me! When I had to call on a particularly long-bottom alcoholic, I sometimes felt actual revulsion.

This honest evaluation of my feelings was as far as I could get. I was filled with guilt and self-loathing because of my attitude. I tried discussing this with one or two other members, but they didn't seem to understand. I finally got to the point where I couldn't tolerate the word "love." Because I thought I could not experience it, I couldn't believe that others could. I called them "phonies." I cried that they were desecrating the word — practicing cheap emotionalism.

I noted that Christ had commanded us to love one another. I reasoned that if it was a commandment, then it must be a thing that could be willed. At this point I decided I must be hopeless. The more I willed it, the more elusive it became.

I have always found beauty in the Prayer of St. Francis of Assisi, have heard it referred to many times in our literature and meetings, and carried a copy of it in my wallet. One day while reading this prayer, the full realization of its meaning began to come through to me. This saintly man was praying to God that it be granted that he seek to love more than to be loved — not that he express love to its fullest, not that he express it at all, not that he seek it completely but only that he seek it more than he sought to be loved.

Hope began to grow in me. I suddenly realized that here was a man, who had lived through the same experience as I, reaching across the centuries to me. The hard core of my guilt began to disintegrate, and there came to my mind what I have always considered as two key words in AA — "willingness" and "grace." I must become willing to seek to love more than I sought to be loved and ask God's grace in granting this. We are our desires. If I began to desire the ability to love, so would it be granted.

Slowly, very slowly, I began to feel a stirring within my soul. Meetings seemed to have a greater depth. I began to feel a new emotion toward the newcomer. Twelfth Step calls were indeed a privilege. I began to feel — love? Could this be love? Yes! I remembered that there are degrees in everything! Because I had not felt the great love for mankind as expressed by a Schweitzer or a Ghandi, I thought I was incapable of any love. The old alcoholic perfectionist!

Now when I attend meetings, it no longer bothers me to hear the members speak of love. I am not sitting alone with guilt and shame. I am sharing, I belong, I am a part of the group. God grant that I may continue to seek not so much to be loved as to love.

Anonymous
Lexington, Kentucky

Miracles to Go
August 1997

I REMEMBER THE BEST AA meeting I ever attended. It was in a western town, a noon meeting in an old building next to the railroad tracks. I was new and not talking yet. I hunkered down on the dilapidated couch, comfortable from years of use, my hat pulled low. Cigarette smoke hung from the ceiling; sunbeams streamed at an angle, landing on a very old wood floor. The coffee was strong.

The meeting began as usual, and a man was called upon to read "How It Works." He began to read very slowly: "Rarely. . .have. . .we. . .seen. . ." I thought, this is going to take forever; they should get another person to read. But they didn't. I looked at the big man slowly struggling to speak each word. His face was scarred and pockmarked. His hands were like mitts. He must have weighed close to three hundred pounds.

One agonizing word after another, and "How It Works" trickled out. The meeting was to end promptly at 1 P.M. It was 12:35, then 12:40. Everyone was silent. No one got up. Forty of us, each had our own thoughts. For the first time I'd noticed how many times the word "honesty" was mentioned in "How It Works."

At 12:45, a wave of something invisible fell over me. I knew I belonged. If there was an answer here for this man, there was going to be one for me. That hour showed me AA at its best — unconditional love and sincere hope that progress in our lives can happen.

At 12:50, the basket came around. The man was still slowly reading. Everyone had tearful eyes, including me.

Who can dispute that a miracle happened that day? This man — who, I learned later, had spent a hard life in prison — finished the last word of "How It Works" at 12:58. We all stood and held hands, and finished simply with the Lord's Prayer.

Norm M.
Cedaredge, Colorado

The Joy of Living

"We are sure God wants us to be happy, joyous, and free."
Alcoholics Anonymous, p. 133

During our drinking days, we imagined not-drinking as a grim, grey, joyless affair. Where would the fun be? The excitement? But we found out that drinking was the grey world; sobriety is in full color. Sobriety offers an abundance of laughter, friendship, the excitement of spiritual and emotional discoveries, and moments of just plain joy. As we grow up and grow out of self-pity and despair, we think no picture of emotional sobriety would be complete if it didn't include the joy.

The Rhythm of Life
October 1998

IN MAY 1993, I ENTERED the Fellowship of Alcoholics Anonymous in the midst of a very painful divorce resulting from years of alcohol abuse on my part. My two children, aged two and three at the time, were caught in the middle of this situation. My recovery went well, and my relationship with my children continued to improve, but after seven months in AA I still felt an absence of peace. Although I'd been working on my spiritual life, I continued to find it difficult to accept the fact that my family was not coming back together. It wasn't long before I started questioning God as to his unwillingness to answer my prayers.

Immediately following my divorce, I was living in a little broken-down trailer. I was broke and I resented the fact that I no longer had a house and all the material things that told me I was okay. Even when I was an emotional and spiritual wreck, my material things had always provided a false sense of being okay. Now I had nothing, and my kids were spending their first weekend in my new home.

I tucked them into bed and went back into the living room and sat in the dark, just thinking and feeling sorry for myself. It had snowed all that day and the full moon was reflected on the freshly fallen snow, illuminating the room with its light. When I got up to go to bed, I stopped in the doorway of the kids' room. I stood there, just watching them sleep. The moonbeams shining through their window cast a beautiful haze upon the bed where they lay sleeping.

What I remember most about that night is the rhythm of their breathing. As the girls slept, I recalled the slow, steady, peaceful rhythm that I marveled at the first time I held them. The same slow, steady, peaceful rhythm was there when I rocked them to sleep in the following years. It was this rhythm that had been a constant for me in my relationship with my children. It was this rhythm that told me they were okay and that in turn my world was okay. It was this rhythm, in an old beat-up trailer in a run-down trailer park, that told me God was listening and my world was okay.

Isn't it interesting the way God whispers to us? But we don't always hear his messages. That's why it's so important for me to work on my relationship with God. I believe the divine to be incarnate in all things, but the only way I know to honor my Higher Power is to talk to him as if he were a person. I never ask him for things anymore, I don't believe he is a genie who grants wishes, but I do believe he gives me strength and hope and an appreciation of life and goodness.

This concept is of great comfort to me, and I think it's what we try to achieve through the spiritual Steps of Alcoholics Anonymous.

Frank K.
Dearborn Heights, Michigan

Hanging in There Together
March 1984

WHEN I CAME ON THE program, in October 1956, it was in a foreign country, where there were no groups, no meeting place, no anything much. A lady passing through Venezuela on a visit carried the message and "captured" five pigeons — three men, me, and one other woman. When our traveling lady departed, she left five very dickery new members. The "oldest" was three months dry. I was last, with a few weeks, barely dry between the ears, still confused, and as nutty as a fruitcake. Our only hope was in hanging in there together, writing a lot of silly, incomprehensible questions to the AA General Service Office. We always got answers. Of course, we knew nothing of treatment centers or recovery homes. We all imagined this was how AA worked: if we wanted to stay sober, we just had to sweat it out. So we sweated and prayed and hung in there.

I'd been drinking for twenty-eight years. Though I desperately wanted what had been offered to me, I had a few slips, overnight storms that drove me insane, fearing I had lost this wonderful new life. But I really wanted sobriety with all my heart and soul. So God gave me other chances. I finally made it back to England, surrendered totally, found a group, and by the grace of God, have been sober since December 28, 1958. Miracles, miracles!

In 1961, when I got to the States and heard about recovery homes and treatment centers, I pooh-poohed the idea. "They'll never make it. You have to do it the hard way; you have to suffer through your own personal crucifixion." Such arrogance! A few years later, I was joyously, happily a housemother in a home for recovering women alcoholics, 1967–69. Some of "my girls" are still sober, and I'm still their loved "auntie."

You may think I'm still nutty as a fruitcake, but I'm so happy, so overjoyed, so everything good, that I'm still on a gorgeous Cloud Nine. Now, that's really something, isn't it? Here I am, nearly seventy-eight, poor as a church mouse, housebound, and partially disabled by a couple of strokes. My floor furnace won't work; neither will my electric fire; and I'm full of the joys of spring, though it looks like snow on the Sandia Mountains. The secret is that I begin my day, every day, with "Good morning, my God. Thank you for a wonderful night's sleep." Thank God for the electric blanket!

Then, I totter out to the kitchen, plug in the coffee, feed "all creatures great and small" (five cats, once strays, now beloved companions, and two dogs, likewise strays and devoted companions). While I'm doing those chores and the coffee is perking, I look out the kitchen window. Again, I could shout my praise and gratitude to God, for sparkling blue skies (they are gray now, and it does look like snow) and for a little apricot tree, a thing of great beauty, glowing golden. Oh, thank God! There's a little story to my apricot tree. It's five or six years old, and it sprouted from a pit I spat out as I walked through the garden on the way to hang out washing. When I saw that little seed, sitting there beside the path, I thought, "Well, God bless you! Maybe if I plant you right here, you will grow." So I did, and it did, and now I have all this beauty. I even had quite a crop of apricots this year!

I am blessed, too, with endless enthusiasm for the Fellowship of AA, with its love, and with the joy of being sober and alive. At a meeting, I give my full name, say I am a recovered alcoholic, give my dry date, and tell the people, "If I can do it, anyone can do it! But you must practice the principles, follow the Steps, get a sponsor, and above all, get active."

I am delighted, when I walk into my group, to hear some of my loved ones say, "Here's old Self-Will Run Riot." Or I may be fondly greeted with "Here's our salty old bitch." I love it, they love me, and all is well. At least, it gives me a sure way of practicing my humility. It is very different from being called "that crazy, drunken bitch," as I was in the old days, isn't it? How good it is to be free of arrogance, sarcasm, lying, and cheating, to be totally honest with myself and my fellowman.

Another little gimmick that keeps me happy and sober is this: if I'm puzzled or anxious about something, I write a little letter to God and tell him all about it. Sometimes, I'm asked, "Aren't you lonely, living by yourself?" Oh, they can't possibly know the joy of solitude, when I can commune with my God as I understand him.

L. P.
Albuquerque, New Mexico

Meetings, Meetings, and More Meetings
March 1995

I HAVE BEEN SOBER FOR twenty-five years. In the peculiar math of Alcoholics Anonymous, twenty-five times 365 equals one. We all share the comradeship of having been sober this one day, which is the only day we really have. But as a friend reminded me a few days ago, "Yeah it's one day at a time — in a row!"

Sobriety has brought with it countless blessings, all of them in the form of people. First there is the continuing relationship with Lynn, my wife of thirty years. Thirty years married and still going. We are the avenue for each other to experience emotions that otherwise we might keep at a safe distance. I've also had the privilege of seeing my children grow up into great human beings who love me, and the birth of grandchildren who also love me.

Why do I keep coming to AA after all these years? One reason is that I laugh here more than anyplace else I go. This laughter is hard to explain, isn't it? We tell each other stories of tragedy and see in our own stories the absurdity of our actions, and we laugh together. I think it's partly relief that allows us to laugh, and partly trust — the laughter comes from knowing that someone else really understands what madness there is in alcoholism. I think also we laugh because we're glad to be alive among a crowd of others equally glad to be alive. This is laughter from heaven.

I also come to AA for the shock of self-recognition. When I hear your stories, I see myself. When I can see myself, I know that I need to be healed, restored, built up and lifted up. I come for the antidote to my own peculiar brand of arrogance, egotism, and pride. This antidote isn't a vaccine but a medicine I require in order to survive these poisons that live inside me. Meetings are where I get this medicine. And you encourage me. I am made brave — that's what "encourage" means, after all — so that I can risk little experiments at being better.

In other words, I come to learn how to be human. The Twelve Steps are a lifelong schooling in what it means to be human. Not for nothing are they called steps: in small increments of improvement that add up over the years, I learn to walk the walk of life together with you. I learn that to be human is to be a creature, that creatures have a Creator; I learn that to be human is to discover the power in powerlessness, to explore the meaning in surrender; I learn to face myself without fear, even with pleasure; I learn to hand over my failings and my successes, to be confessional and vulnerable, to live in the day, for the day's failings and successes are enough for human beings. I learn to deepen my relationship with God, and to carry the message to other alcoholics.

And I come for friendship and affection — not only the friendly and affectionate feelings of others toward me although I treasure them, but for the inspiration you give me to feel friendly and affectionate toward you. This is harder for me: to invest myself in others.

It's a characteristic of all humans, not just drunks, either to be on their way toward the best that is in them or the worst. There's no such thing as standing still. I'm either getting better or I'm getting worse. I can't content myself with indulging a little bit of badness, because it will progress. I will become a bit more bad as I age, and a bit more, and more, until by the time I'm old I will have become all of what I only indulged in at forty, but relished at fifty, and was consumed by at sixty. Allowing myself to love you, admitting to myself that I would miss you if you should die — these are ways of continuing my growth without which something much worse than death happens to me: I become that which I loathe within me. A little liar become The Liar. A little thief becomes The Thief. A little sadist becomes the Marquis. A little whiner becomes The Total Self-Pitier. You protect me from my wicked self and lift up the image of my good self for me to keep striving after. For this, I am indebted to you. For this, I love you, and I will miss you if you die.

So, in summation, this is why I continue to come to meetings:

I come for sobriety.

I come to keep up my gratitude and subdue my taking-for-granted-tude.

I come because this is where I laugh more than anywhere else.

I come for the shock of self-recognition.

I come for the antidote to pride.

I come to learn how to be human.

I come to learn how to love.

What keeps me coming to meetings after twenty-five years is certainly necessity, but necessity never did anything for me as a motivating force. It was pleasure that has always motivated me, and that is still the bottom line: I come for the pleasure of it, the pure pleasure.

Anonymous
Irasburg, Vermont

Practical Joy

February 1997

R ECENTLY, THE HARD WORK my wife and I have put in has been
bearing rewards of modest material security: new house, new car, money to buy Christmas gifts and maintain a prudent reserve, and more prospects
for creative work. Though we've been working for these things for several
years, they've come quite suddenly in the last month. Our house plans have
turned out especially well. So I enjoy telling AA friends that I spent time praying about the situation, and that what we've ended up with is not at all what I
dreamed about and planned for — it's better.

People in the Fellowship have a special warmth when you share good news
with them. We've all experienced so much bitterness, loss, and grief when
drinking that any affirmation of life turning out well in sobriety gives our
nervous systems a tingle of hope.

However, I cringe at AA meetings when I hear people claiming that their
modest or great good fortune is a result of prayer: "When my car broke down
I prayed for God's will to be done. And the next day my Uncle Bill called and
offered me his old car for free." Over and over at meetings I hear variations on
this version of how prayer works in people's lives, as though this were proof
that God gives us what we need.

God is not Santa Claus, I want to shout in reply. Prayer and meditation are
not application forms to some cosmic welfare program. The Promises don't
say a thing about getting back any of the stuff we lost to drinking. I know because I lost everything: property, money, business — everything. In fact, my net
worth in sobriety has never equaled what it was in my drinking days.

My reaction is a signpost flagging my need for an inventory, of course. The
intellectual arrogance that made me a know-it-all drunk hasn't miraculously
vanished in sobriety, in spite of fervent prayer to have it removed. But I still
believe that, as our Third and Eleventh Steps insist, prayer and meditation are
intensely practical. Just as these Steps claim, I was convinced of the effective-

ness of prayer by the results I saw in my life. But this was years before I began earning back some of the material things I lost to alcoholism.

I was two years sober before I was able to recognize how prayer had been working in my life from the beginning. When I came to AA, I had no Higher Power and no clue why I needed one. What I did have was an overpowering obsession to drink that I could no longer control. My sponsor told me it would help if I prayed to have the obsession removed. So, without having any faith in what I was doing, I prayed. I also did a lot of other things my sponsor suggested. But only because I wanted the insane urge to drink to go away. My mental obsession with booze was a daily battle for almost two years.

What I could see when the obsession finally diminished was that, despite a lifetime of defiant self-sufficiency, I'd had the willingness to ask for help and then follow someone else's suggestions. This was new. I prayed daily for help with the obsession, and was given the willingness to follow directions — something I'd never had before.

I saw too that I'd been given perseverance and stamina. When this didn't yield instant results, instead of jumping track the way I had in almost everything else in my life, I continued working the Steps one day at a time. I'd always worked hard but I'd rarely stuck with any one thing very long. This was new to me too.

I began to have some genuine trust in my AA friends and sponsor. I'd never trusted anyone before, and with good reason: I thought everyone was at least as untrustworthy as me! But I was given self-acceptance. I came to see that, like everyone, I made mistakes, and that this was not reason to dislike, shun, or manipulate people. I came to rely on the fact that other people could and would help me. And I saw and trusted other people's good intentions. When I began conducting my business affairs on this basis, I saw success returning to them.

And even during the sober years when my finances were bouncing below the poverty line, I learned to be grateful for the simple life and friends and hopes that I had. After all, I'd come from a place where I had only the chaos and impending doom of active alcoholism. So I learned about the place of gratitude: the importance of recognizing that the gifts in my life were not of my own making. I did the footwork. But the results were up to God.

Beyond working the Twelve Steps, I've never understood what God's will is for me. I see that my Higher Power didn't give me the material things I thought I needed and wanted and deserved in life. My Higher Power gave me the emotional and spiritual tools I'd need to acquire these things, and also gave me the choice of where and whether or not I wanted to use these tools.

This is all in the Steps. And it's a lot more than I had when I was drinking, even though — in financial terms — I owned more then than I do now. If I hadn't been given the willingness to follow a sponsor's directions in the beginning and pray simply because he thought it was a good idea, I still would have no idea how to use the rest of the tool kit. Possibly I might have acquired the house and car and loving companion that I have today. But given the attitude I had when drinking, these gifts could have only inspired a sense of emptiness.

I still have moments like that. Well, so I have some nice things again — so what? I still feel empty and lost. What's the point? A dry drunk.

The gift today is that I have an immediate answer for that attitude. I get it every time I call an AA friend, read AA literature, talk to an AA newcomer, do AA service work, or pray. The point is to pass it on.

So now I have the means and the joy to carry the message. And what I see in retrospect is that I've had the means ever since my first sober day in AA, even when I was living on food stamps and had to borrow money during my seventh sober year. The joy was always available too. But I didn't know enough to pray for that. I had to be sober longer before I understood the practical aspect of joy. Not the joy of owning. The joy of living. To me, this is the Great Reality of Alcoholics Anonymous.

Ernest S.
York Harbor, Maine

Savoring Our Sobriety
August 1982

IT WAS NATURAL FOR US to begin our journey of happy sobriety in Alcoholics Anonymous with an anticipation of trouble in trying to live in the now, one day at a time. After all, we had spent years deeply regretting painful pasts and weeping about dismal futures.

We are fortunate that so much attention is directed during AA meetings at the importance of making life a matter of today's concern — not yesterday's nor tomorrow's. If we forget that growth is achieved one step at a time, we are doomed to flounder in confusion.

I came to AA as an agnostic. What, besides the bottle, did I have to believe in while drinking? I was started on my understanding of a Higher Power by hearing that God has time only for each today as it comes.

If God does not exist in yesterday or tomorrow, then we can be at peace with our conception of God only during the now. If we choose to retrogress into the past or project into the future, we'll be alone in our thinking, since God is not to be found in such areas. And the loneliness of stinking thinking is all too familiar to alcoholics.

Living in the present rids us of both guilt and fear. Guilt can materialize only from an errant past and fear from intrusions on unknown futures. Resentments develop only from what has already been felt and fear from apprehension about experiences yet to be confronted.

If we are to find spiritual growth and serenity, we must dress our minds each morning as carefully as we dress our bodies. Only then can today become the glorious tomorrow we looked forward to yesterday.

Because each of us, at any moment, is the sum total of every choice he or she has ever made, it is not sheer fantasy to expect each day to be the best day we have yet lived. There surely never will be a wreckage in the future as devastating as what we encountered when we were guzzlers — so long as we stay sober.

At some point in each today, we recovering alcoholics need to pay ourselves a friendly visit. Ultimately, at our individual paces, we will get to know ourselves. Some AA members go so far as to contend that an unexamined day may hardly be worth living (to paraphrase Plato).

Today's sobriety cannot be chugalugged like alcohol. It has to be sipped, one taste at a time, so that each drop of serenity can be fully savored. It is well to remember that nothing can replace persistence as a tool for sobriety — not talent, genius, nor education.

When we alcoholics concentrate on living only one day at a time, we find that the best gift of any day is a fuller understanding of values. The things that count cease being those that can be held in the hand and become only what can be held in the heart. Hence, none of our real gifts can be stolen from us. We can lose them only through our own carelessness and complacency.

It is a tough job for most of us to avoid procrastination. Of course, procrastination does not belong in one-day-at-a-time living. We must avoid the use of the word "should." In AA growth, it is a put-off-until-tomorrow word, an indefinite word that accomplishes nothing. It invites rationalization. It is best that we substitute the word "will." "I will do . . ." rather than "I should do . . ."

Our program assures us that all answers to our daily problems are found in living in the now. Solutions that worked for yesterday's woes might be outmoded today. And reaching into the future for answers is wishful thinking.

Perhaps all of the living-today lessons we learn in AA can be boiled down into this often-made quip: a sober alcoholic who has one eye on yesterday and the other on tomorrow is likely to be cockeyed today.

C. C.
North Hollywood, California

Savoring Sobriety

August 1997

URING MY DRINKING DAYS, my life was in free fall. I didn't think before I acted, didn't accept responsibility, didn't show up, didn't behave morally or decently. To rationalize this behavior, I presented myself to myself and others as a free spirit and a hedonist. I really thought I was a pleasure-seeker when in fact I was merely seeking gratification for my addiction to alcohol. I didn't see that my "free-spirited" behaviors — my selfishness, the carelessness of my love life, my lack of commitment, the wild unmanageability of my life — weren't choices, but came directly out of my alcoholism and my desire to evade reality. I had to see myself as a hedonist because I couldn't claim more solid accomplishments; there was in fact very little true pleasure or contentment in my life. How could there be when I didn't have any peace of mind?

Several weeks after I walked into my first AA meeting — a Monday night beginners meeting in New York City — I saw my first copy of the Grapevine. I'd already started to read the Big Book, the "Twelve and Twelve," and Living Sober. Now I was looking at the cover on that August 1982 Grapevine, and I saw this short headline: "Savoring Our Sobriety." I never thought I'd savor anything except bourbon, and here was this wonderful little magazine, which I'd never heard of before, saying, Yes, sobriety can be savored. And the Grapevine was right.

What does it mean to me to truly savor a sober life? The most important thing is that I'm in the present moment, not in the past or future; it means I don't speed by my life so fast it's just a blur; it means being quiet in my mind and not worrying about things I can't solve today or conducting conversations and arguments with people who aren't in the room. I often have to remind myself to slow down and stay in the moment. I live in Manhattan, where the preferred mode of existence is faster (cities gave us the term "rush hour," after all), and in the rush and the hurry I sometimes forget to breathe. Just last night, as I was walking down Broadway after work, I had to make myself stop to look at the evening sky and the last light fading on the tall buildings, take a deep breath from my belly, count my breaths from one to ten, and recall that life wasn't going to start sometime in the future: the moment was now to relax, breathe, look around me, be alive. Don't clench; don't grab; slow down. "Easy Does It" is very simple and very useful. Also useful is a small prayer or affirmation: please let me wear the world as a loose garment.

Something else I must do to savor sobriety is try to accept other people, even ones I disagree with or dislike, even the most long-winded sharer in my home group or the person I've heard complain a million times (haven't I tested my group's patience?). I can't savor sobriety when I'm imprisoned by "self-centered fear," so that means making a phone call to a friend, or saying hello to a newcomer, or making a point to sit next to somebody at a meeting and catch up with what's going on with them. No big deals, just simple things.

When I slow down I can take pleasure in the many good things of this world: good conversation, books, music, making a meal for a friend, taking a walk, watching a movie, having a quiet cup of tea. My husband (who is also an AA member) is an actor, and I like classical music, so we've combined our interests into an appreciation for opera and have season tickets to an opera company which is located up the street from us. Seven or eight times a year, we get dressed up and go out to dinner and then sit in orchestra seats in one of the world's great opera houses, waiting happily for the moment when the house lights dim and the starburst chandeliers rise to the ceiling and the orchestra begins the overture. What a treat! We never fail to enjoy ourselves or to appreciate the fact that we're sitting there sober; we don't take it for granted for a moment. Recently, we were enjoying a pre-opera dinner when I said to my husband, "You know, we couldn't enjoy this so much if we didn't also enjoy going out for coffee after our home group meetings." How could I enjoy the big-ticket items in my life if I didn't enjoy the little things? It's not even a matter of "big" and "little" — everything's part of a continuum. The 13th century Zen master Dogen said that a cook must prepare a simple broth of wild grasses with the same care that he prepares a rich cream soup. Savoring comes from paying attention to the task at hand, whatever it is.

I think that's where gratitude comes in: to help me to better appreciate whatever is going on in my life. Gratitude isn't a duty I have to perform, it's a tool, a form of perspective. It reminds me to appreciate the simple things: every night that I go to bed sober and not in a blackout, every morning that I wake up without a hangover.

There's a nice chapter in the story that began fifteen years ago: today I'm a member of the editorial staff here at the Grapevine. This means that for the past several years I've been part of a team that puts the magazine together and gets it into the hands of over 125,000 readers around the world. Somewhere right now, this month, a new member of AA is reading the Grapevine for the first time. And I want her to know: sobriety can be savored. This is the gift we've been given: a real life that grows more vivid and more interesting and offers more to be enjoyed and relished and delighted in. I hope that if you are a first-time reader of the Grapevine, the magazine will continue to be your companion on the journey. It's one of the ways that many of us savor our sobriety—and it always reminds me how lucky I am to have a life worth slowing down for.

Anonymous
New York, New York

The Man I've Always Wanted to Be
October 1990

IN NOVEMBER 1977, DURING ONE of my many stays "around" the program, an Al-Anon member asked me why I wouldn't work AA's Twelve Steps. In all sincerity I told him, "I don't need the Steps to stay sober. The Fellowship of AA is enough to keep me sober." I kept slippin' and slidin' around the meetings, convinced I had this AA business all figured out.

Two months later I took what turned out to be my last drink, although I didn't know that at the time. Shortly afterward I was in a beginner's meeting, for people with less than a year of sobriety, where the topic was AA's Twelve Steps. The chairperson called on the man seated next to me, and what he said helped change my life.

This fellow was a loudmouthed, obnoxious, self-promoter who invariably took up meeting time to talk about cars, business, and anything except sobriety. He had been "around" the program for nineteen years. I despised him heartily. Imagine my surprise, then, when he puffed out his chest, folding his arms across a flabby gut, and said, "I don't need the Steps to stay sober. The Fellowship of AA is enough to keep me sober."

You might say it was a sobering experience to hear my words coming from that mouth. I looked at him and said to myself, "I don't want to be like you!" Here was a guy who'd been "around" for nineteen years, saying the same thing I'd said just two months earlier! I really did not want to be like him!

Fortunately, I had an option. A group in our town was known as a very Step-oriented, hard-core bunch with a lot of strong old-time sobriety, and that's where I went. I don't believe it was a conscious decision, but I knew those folks were different from some AA people I'd met, and I wanted to become as "different" from that loudmouthed fellow as was humanly possible. I attended the meetings for a while, and finally found a man I wanted as my sponsor. He seemed the opposite of the loudmouth, with a quiet grace and gentle manner that appealed to me. What really hooked me, though, were his frequent references to caring for a nephew who'd recently lost his mother in a car wreck. That touched me, so I worked up the nerve and asked him to sponsor me.

Never let anyone tell you that God doesn't have a sense of humor. The man I selected as sponsor was a short, rotund businessman who drove a huge Lincoln and, for some reason, hated bikers. I'm a long-time Harley fanatic who, for some reason, hated short, fat, rich cats in fancy cars. Hence we were perfect for each other.

The first thing my sponsor told me was, "I don't have time to help you stay sick — I'm much too busy for that — but if you want to get better I'd be glad to help."

He definitely meant what he said, but my sponsor was not one of these head-crackin' types that order their pigeons about. That was just as well, because I was extremely rebellious when I sobered up, and could have seized on a domineering sponsor as an excuse to chuck it all and return to drinking. Instead, my sponsor laid out a set of tools (the Twelve Steps) and told me how he used them in his life. There were no demands made of me. He simply said, "If you want what we have, come and get it," and that's what I needed to hear.

Through my sponsor, and other members, I've learned that this program offers much more than simple dry time. They not only told me about, but actually lived, what I now know as the Promises. They explained that the Promises were an end result of working the Steps to the best of my ability, and that life in AA took on a whole new definition when compared with the miserable existence I'd known out on the streets.

My friends did not lie. I have done more, accomplished more, learned more, and gone farther in the past thirteen years than all the other years of my life put together. One of my favorite words, when I came to AA, was freedom, but my concept of freedom was limited. I thought it meant doing what I pleased, when I pleased, without regard for consequences. Now I am truly free: to walk through any given day or situation without cringing in fear, exploding in rage, getting loaded, or self-destructing; to love, laugh, and know and appreciate the simple joys that come with being alive; to be a part of, instead of apart from, a society where I can serve an invaluable purpose; to recognize and utilize my own talents and abilities, as a writer, a worker, husband, stepfather and participating member in the Fellowship of Alcoholics Anonymous. I'm free to be the man I've always wanted to be, but never before had the courage to become.

In what I see as a prime representation of AA's magic, I was offered two examples situated at opposite ends of sobriety's spectrum. Adrift between the two poles, I was blessed with a clear-cut choice, and for that I'm very grateful. I needed something just that black-and-white to penetrate the stone wall of excuses I'd built around myself. I now know, and my life in sobriety has proven to me, that I've made the right choice.

I'm also pleased to report that my sponsor has gotten over his hatred for motorcyclists, while I've mellowed somewhat in my distaste for short, fat, rich folks. As for the loudmouth? Maybe he found his own examples, because at last count he had several years of continuous sobriety, and was still going strong.

Wm. J.
Temple, Texas

A Twig In the Yard
July 2001

Bill M., sent us the following note along with a letter from his son, who is serving time in Kernersville, North Carolina

"THIS IS A STORY ABOUT GRATITUDE — gratitude in an unlikely setting. My son is halfway through a long prison sentence, the beginning of which marked a deep bottom in his life and the beginning of his recovery from alcoholism. He now serves as a peer counselor in a state-run program that struggles to make sobriety available in the prison environment. His growth and his Twelfth Step work constantly amaze me. A recent letter was so striking that I asked his permission to share it with you and your readers. It began with the news that he had finally been able to see a dentist — no small feat when it requires that he be transported a hundred miles to a prison facility that had such resources."

Dear Dad,

Yesterday at 4:00 A.M. I was awakened in order to be taken to the dentist. It was the first time in a year that I'd been outside for a ride, so I was really excited. Of course, I had to be handcuffed to a waist chain, then shackled before I could get in the van. The van was brand-new: the smell was delicious and the seat was so comfortable. I must have looked like a dog out for a drive, staring eagerly from side to side. It was amazing to be moving — and in such comfort.

When we got to the facility, they took off my chains and let me walk around the prison yard. I got to touch a tree for the first time in over three years! It was an oak tree, and the bark felt so good beneath my hand. I looked up through the branches and leaves to the sun shining through. The ground was littered with small twigs and real acorns that crunched beneath my feet. The trunk, which must have been seven or eight feet around, was covered with moss and lichens. I have never seen a more beautiful sight.

As if that were not enough, a calico cat suddenly rubbed up against my leg and gave me permission to pet him while he drank from a water dish. I was dumbstruck with all the sensation. The feel of bark and cat fur, the sight of open space and green leaves — all this for a man who'd had none of them for years — were for me what climbing Mt. Everest must be to a free man. Then it ended. We left after my visit to the dentist, yet I will always carry that day with me as a symbol of God's grace and as a reminder to have gratitude for the small, mundane things of everyday life.

A twig in the yard — what joy! I'm so glad to have you to share it with. I don't think anyone else would understand.

– Your son

Alcoholics Anonymous

AA'S PROGRAM OF RECOVERY IS fully set forth in its basic text, *Alcoholics Anonymous* (commonly known as the Big Book), now in its Fourth Edition, as well as in *Twelve Steps and Twelve Traditions* and other books. Information on AA can also be found on AA's website at www.aa.org, or by writing to: Alcoholics Anonymous, Box 459, Grand Central Station, New York, NY 10163. For local resources, check your local telephone directory under "Alcoholics Anonymous."

The AA Grapevine

THE GRAPEVINE IS AA'S INTERNATIONAL monthly journal, published continuously since its first issue in June 1944. The AA pamphlet on the Grapevine describes its scope and purpose this way: "As an integral part of Alcoholics Anonymous for more than sixty years, the Grapevine publishes articles that reflect the full diversity of experience and thought found within the AA fellowship. No one viewpoint of philosophy dominates its pages, and in determining content, the editorial staff relies on the principles of the Twelve Traditions."

In addition to a monthly magazine, the Grapevine also produces anthologies, audiocassette tapes and audioCDs based on published articles, an annual wall calendar, and a pocket planner. The entire collection of Grapevine articles is available online in its Digital Archive. AA Grapevine also publishes La Viña, AA's Spanish-language magazine.

For more information on the Grapevine, or to subscribe, please visit the magazine's website at www.aagrapevine.org or write to:

The AA Grapevine
475 Riverside Drive
New York, NY 10115
You may also call:

English	1-800-631-6025 (US)
	1-800-734-5856 (International)
Spanish	1-800-640-8781 (US)
	1-800-734-5857 (International)

E-mail: gvcirculation@aagrapevine.org